The Meaning of Missional

The Meaning of Missional

*A Beginner's Guide to Missional Living
and the Missional Church*

Dick Wiedenheft

FOREWORD BY
Mike Breen

WIPF & STOCK · Eugene, Oregon

THE MEANING OF MISSIONAL
A Beginner's Guide to Missional Living and the Missional Church

Wipf & Stock
An Imprint of Wipf and Stock Publishers
199 W. 8th Ave., Suite 3
Eugene, OR 97401

www.wipfandstock.com

PAPERBACK ISBN: 978-1-5326-6028-3
HARDCOVER ISBN: 978-1-5326-6029-0
EBOOK ISBN: 978-1-5326-6030-6

Contents

Foreword

DOING MISSION DEPENDS UPON being missional, and being missional depends upon a deep appreciation of the priority and importance of God's mission to the world.

When I say *the priority and importance of God's mission,* what I mean is that being missional is not a subset of being a Christian; rather, being a Christian is entirely dependent upon someone being *on mission* towards us, and that *someone* is, of course, God himself. God is on a mission to the world, a mission that is seen perfectly in the person of Jesus Christ and made manifest in his church in every age.

God's mission is the reason we became a Christian in the first place. This is important because our faith does not give birth to mission; mission—God's mission—gives birth to us (Eph 2:1–10).

If mission is the origin of our faith as Christians, then it must also be the reason the church exists at all. Grasping this is often a matter of perspective. If you entered the court of Rameses, the Pharaoh of Egypt in Exodus chapter 2, and asked someone what was Jochebed's status within the royal court, you would have been told that she was either the servant of the adopted prince, Moses, or the handmaid of Pharaoh's daughter. But this answer, though true on the surface, would have hidden a much deeper truth—Jochebed was the mother of Moses.

 Mission is the mother of the church; without it the community of believers would not exist. And so, understanding the *meaning of missional* is not an obscure pursuit reserved for the very academic or deeply committed . . . it is something that all of us need to grasp if we are to understand the foundation of our faith and the purpose of the church.

A realization of this truth has catapulted the missional conversation from the margins of theological speculation into the mainstream of Christian communication. But, if truth be told, this has not always resulted in deeper understanding or greater clarity.

Commenting on the sudden emergence of the missional conversation, Alan Roxburgh has said:

> "In a very brief period of time, a new form of language entered the common conversation of the church and diffused itself across all forms of church life at the same time; it is still not understood by the vast majority of people in either leadership or the pew. This is a stunning accomplishment, from obscurity to banality in . . . (a few) short years."[1]

Of course, *mission* is important—vitally important—and that means we all need to better understand how to think about it and how to put it into practice. But for most of us, the word "missional" is found somewhere between obscurity and banality—somewhere between being talked about too much and talked about too little. And perhaps it is an intuitive appreciation of this fact that has discouraged many of us from pursuing a greater understanding of its meaning and significance.

But . . . here is a book that can really help! Rooted in the practical application of contemporary mission, it not only rescues us from the tyranny of the obscurity/banality continuum—providing clarity where there was once obscurity and significance where there was once banality—but, more importantly, it offers multiple ways of putting into practice what we learn.

If you desire to better understand the *meaning of missional*, my suggestion is that you start here.

—Mike Breen
August 2018

1. Roxburgh, "Missional Church," 2, edits mine.

Acknowledgments

I WOULD LIKE TO thank Robert Neely, Libby and Gavin Culmer, and Mike and Sally Breen, as well as everyone at Wipf and Stock Publishers, for their support, input, and encouragement in bringing this book to publication. I am also grateful to Sarah Grace and Darlene Wiedenheft for proofreading the manuscript and for their editorial insights. Thanks also to Al Giles for his encouragement and to him, Tim McIntyre, Caesar and Tina Kalinowski, as well as Gina Mueller, Stephanie Williams O'Brien, Heidi Macias, Paul Maconochie and many others in the 3DM movement for their partnership in learning how to live missionally. I would also like to thank the two churches I have had the privilege of pastoring for patiently allowing me to figure out what it looks like to be a pastor today and to live and lead missionally. Finally, I would like to thank my dear wife Anne for her unending love and encouragement. *Soli Deo Gloria.*

Introduction

WHAT DOES IT MEAN to be missional? Missional has become a buzzword in recent years, and I have heard this question come up in gatherings of pastors, in church leadership meetings, and in casual conversations.

For example, several years ago I sat in a brown bag lunch with several local pastors, and the topic turned to what this new term "missional" meant. Those around the table compared their understandings. One told how a new church claiming to be missional had recently begun in his town. From what he had observed of them, he concluded that missional meant getting rid of programs and being relational and organic instead. Another pastor thought missional just meant having a solid church-wide commitment to evangelism. He could not see what all the fuss was about—didn't every church already know this was important? A third thought missional was related to that "young people's 'emerging church' thing." He figured the younger generation would get over their attraction to couches and candles once they matured a bit. I then took a deep breath and tried to explain that missional is much more than any of these things.

Because missional involves a fundamental paradigm shift and a wholesale reorientation to what church is and how we function together as God's people, explaining it in a couple minutes is not an easy task. I have often found that the best I can do in a short conversation is to help people realize that within the concept of missional lie significant, profound, and important discoveries.

Last summer I had one such conversation with a representative from the seminary I attended. She described how her local church was struggling to connect with its surrounding community in relevant and meaningful ways. The church members felt stuck and frustrated, and she sensed that they needed help thinking outside the box. As I described how my church is learning to be missional in our posture toward our local community, she was eager to learn more.

After such conversations, I have often wished I could hand people like this young woman a book that provides a clear explanation of what being missional means and why it is so important. What I have found, however, is that most books on the subject suffer from one of two shortcomings. One type of book is too dense and theologically technical to be appreciated by most Christians. These books could leave the false impression that missional thinking is esoteric and impractical. The other type of book tends to be written by young tattooed church planters who hang out in pubs. While there is plenty to admire about this second group of authors, many of my congregants and ministerial colleagues might not relate to them or perhaps even respect them. These books could leave the false impression that a missional approach is only for the young and edgy.

For these reasons, I have attempted to write a book on the meaning of missional which is readable and widely accessible. It seems to me that such a book is necessary because the compelling and urgent message of the missional movement has still not been clearly grasped by the broader church. As missional expert Caesar Kalinowski observed in a blog post entitled "Who Broke the Missional Movement?", " . . . despite all of the hype and all of the 'cool-factor' connected to this hoped-for movement, most pastors and leaders I know have still barely embraced a lifestyle of discipleship and mission."[2] I hope this book will help many to gain greater clarity on what it means to be missional, why becoming missional is so important, and how to begin your own missional journey

---

2. Kalinowski, "Missional Movement?", para. 8.

As you read, you will notice that the book moves from the theoretical to the practical. In chapter 1, I begin with my own journey toward embracing missional thinking. Chapter 2 then seeks to show how missional theology is woven into the very fabric of the Bible. Chapter 3 explores the recent changes in Western culture which have caused the missional movement to become popular (and necessary) now. In chapters 4 and 5, I seek to clear up misconceptions and to explain exactly what missional means. Then, in chapter 6, I describe the costs of becoming missional and also point out the costs of not doing so. Finally, in chapter 7, I conclude with some first steps readers can take to experience for themselves what becoming missional entails. At the end of each chapter, questions are provided for small group discussion or individual reflection. Those who are "doers" may want to begin in chapters 4 or 5 to get a sense of what becoming missional looks like on the ground, before returning to the earlier chapters to consider how important becoming missional is.

I am convinced that to live missionally is to live the way Christ intended. It is to live out our identity and our calling as God's people. I long for the day when those who are missional are no longer just a movement within Christianity. My yearning is that the Christian church will return to its roots, where living together on God's mission is simply what it means to be Christian. It is my prayer that this book provides the clarity and inspiration needed to grasp this vision and the practical tools necessary to begin this exciting journey.

CHAPTER 1

A Pastor's Story

I STILL REMEMBER THE moment it struck me. I was fidgeting in an armchair while the adults in the living room discussed the Bible and spent time in prayer. As I sat half-listening, it dawned on me. They did not believe half of what the Bible said. They marveled at how the boy David had courageously defeated the giant Goliath with only a few stones and a sling. Yet, they did not seem willing to take any audacious risks for God themselves. They read about the many miracles performed by Moses, Elijah, Jesus, and the apostles. Still, their prayers safely avoided putting God in a position where he would have to do anything big. They discussed Jesus's command to go to all nations and make disciples, and they enjoyed the inspiring story of how the early church took up this task. However, as far as I could tell, they felt little compulsion to speak to their friends or neighbors about Jesus. From the way these church folks discussed God's word and then talked to God in prayer, it was clear to me that they trusted God for very little and sought his help mainly to resolve their personal problems. Then and there as a junior high kid, I decided I could not believe in Jesus until someone could show me he was real.

Thankfully, several years later I stepped onto a college campus and met several young people whose lives demonstrated the reality of Jesus. These students were passionate for Christ, bold in sharing their faith, and earnest in expecting their Lord to transform every aspect of their lives. This was the life the Bible had described. It was real after all, and I wanted it! I immediately joined the campus fellowship group to which these newfound friends belonged, and I committed my own life to Christ. A new adventure was beginning to unfold.

By my senior year of college, these friends and I had devoted countless hours to sharing our faith, reaching out on campus, and discipling fellow students in the ways of Jesus. We had also gone on summer mission trips where we became aware that there was a whole world out there in need of poverty relief, justice, education, and the good news about Jesus. We had watched graduating seniors from our fellowship head off to drill wells in Cambodia, provide counseling services in Tanzania, plant churches in Papua New Guinea, and start college fellowships on other campuses. Following Jesus was proving to be an amazing adventure. It demanded our complete commitment, but in return, it offered us purpose, joy, and contentment. We had experienced God personally and seen God work powerfully. Our lives were being transformed in ways we could never have even anticipated.

During those college years, one of the few times I felt disheartened in my newfound faith was when I went to church. I did not experience this every time I went, but often enough. On Sunday mornings, a few friends and I would pile into a friend's car and dutifully head off to a local congregation. We had been told by some older Christians that our on-campus fellowship was a parachurch ministry and was only meant to supplement God's real priority, the local church. Yet, when we walked into church we were often sorely disappointed. The sermons we heard and the people we met often reminded me of those house-church Bible studies I had attended growing up. They were polite, warm, and "Bible-based," but I sensed little of the vibrant spiritual reality I was experiencing on campus.

When it was my turn to graduate, I had several job offers before me. I chose the one which I felt would challenge me most spiritually. That August, I boarded a plane for Budapest, Hungary to teach English in a public high school there. These were the days right after Communism had fallen, and the Christian service organization with which I had signed on was advertising that Eastern and Central Europe were "wide open for the gospel." What an exciting time to become a missionary! However, I had much to learn about what mission involves.

As my two American teammates and I settled into our new home in a foreign land, we quickly learned that living as missionaries requires focus and intentionality. Believe it or not, it was easy to forget why we were there. Despite sacrificing other opportunities and traveling to a far-off country, many diversions threatened to distract us from our purpose.

First, because there were many other missionaries in the city, it was tempting to surround ourselves with other American Christians. Then, there were the daily challenges of learning to live in a foreign culture, to communicate in a difficult language, to navigate an unfamiliar city, and to plan lessons and grade homework. Additionally, there were exciting opportunities to explore the treasures of Hungarian culture, to travel Europe, and to find romance (after all, we were in our twenties!).

At least we found accountability in the monthly prayer letter we needed to write to those back home and in the retreats our organization held which reminded us why we were there. Still, it took time for us to develop and internalize our identity as missionaries and then to live that out faithfully and consistently every day. How much harder it is for those who live their Christian life in their own culture to remember that we have all been sent on a mission.

Another important lesson my teammates and I learned about mission is well illustrated by my experience with two of our senior classes. When we first arrived at the school to which we had been assigned, the principal sat us down and told us that years of Communism had left his students without any moral or spiritual foundation. He welcomed us to share our religion with the students!

In our excitement to seize this opportunity, we made a mistake soon thereafter. A short-term mission team from another missions organization came to town, and we hastily arranged for them to visit our classes one afternoon. They played Christian rock music for our students and shared the gospel message. One senior class who experienced this afternoon responded with resentment at being forced to listen to this religious presentation. For the rest of the school year, they were resistant to the subject of Jesus.

By contrast, another senior class did not have English class that afternoon. Near the end of the school year, I realized that my teammates and I had shared our faith with several of them and that the class had observed all year how my teammates and I related to them and each other. However, I had never told everyone in the class what I believed. During the last week of class, I asked the class for permission to share my beliefs with them, and they happily agreed. As I shared the good news about Jesus with them, they listened with interest and appreciation. Thus, I learned the importance of building relationships of trust and earning the right to speak about my beliefs. If this is necessary even with those who are relatively open to the gospel, how much more so with those who are less open.

Another memorable experience occurred when I first met some missionaries representing the Alliance for Saturation Church Planting. Their vision was to see multiplying movements of church plants catalyzed in countries throughout the region, until every village and neighborhood in these countries had its own local church as a gospel witness. The audacity of this vision blew me away. Yet, it seemed like exactly what a God who can do "immeasurably more than all we ask or imagine" (Eph 3:20) would desire. They explained that such movements were already well underway in a number of developing countries. They also commented that aside from encouraging signs in a few cities, nothing like this was gaining traction in the United States. Americans, they explained, expect churches to include so many bells and whistles that churches cannot be multiplied nearly quickly enough to begin a movement.

These are just a few of the stories I could tell about how my teammates and I grew and were stretched as we learned to be missionaries. We met fellow missionaries and other Christians from many countries and backgrounds. We struggled to learn the Hungarian language and culture, to contextualize the gospel in ways which resonated with the students, and to disciple the kids who came to Christ. We battled culture shock, loneliness, and conflicts among ourselves (the stresses of missionary work brought out some ugly aspects of our characters). Through these adventures and challenges, our faith became deeper, stronger, and more resilient. Our Christian lives would never be the same.

After three years in Budapest, I still wanted to devote my life to God's mission, but I figured out that I was not well suited for cross-cultural service. My gifts, I sensed, could be better used in my own country. When I returned to the States, I joined a friend of a friend who was planting a multiethnic church in our nation's capital. To support myself, I found a job at a non-profit that addressed local hunger and poverty concerns in the District of Columbia. These new endeavors provided plenty of additional lessons and opportunities to stretch and grow my faith.

One lesson I learned again was how easily God's people can get distracted from our mission. The church plant core team, of which I was part, faced a constant temptation to bypass the evangelism and community outreach efforts we felt called to do. For one thing, we lived in a city that attracts a steady stream of newcomers, and a certain percentage of them are already responsible and dependable Christians. How much easier it would be to build a church by attracting these folks, rather than by doing the slow and often messy work of investing in our local community and discipling those who came to know Jesus.

Additionally, many of our team were more comfortable doing ministry inside the church than we were reaching those outside of it. Starting a new church gave us plenty to do, and it was easy to procrastinate the less familiar task of reaching out. Unless we were intentional, we were in danger of starting yet another inwardly focused church which ultimately had little impact on those around it.

Another major lesson I learned during this time was the importance of being present with, and among, those we are seeking to reach. My job, church plant involvement, and social life placed me in several very different worlds. My job was unique in that I straddled both the halls of power and the mean streets of the inner city. One day I might be wearing a suit to a meeting on Capitol Hill, and the next day a T-shirt and jeans in a local soup kitchen. I quickly learned that a successful lobbyist has different concerns and hears the gospel quite differently than a recovering addict does. I came to realize that the middle-class African-American professionals who were part of our church plant had very different experiences than the African-Americans who visited local food pantries. Meanwhile, I worked and hung out mostly with young white singles who worked in the city but lived in the suburbs.

As a church plant core team member, I felt a big responsibility to invite people to our church plant. Yet, I could not imagine most of the young suburban singles or the homeless and recovering addicts I spent much of my time with feeling comfortable in our fledgling church that was composed mainly of middle-class families. In addition, many of those I could invite did not live anywhere near the church. I was just not meeting the kind of people our church plant was seeking to reach.

My job presented further lessons about the importance of presence and proximity in mission. In the course of my work, I listened to politicians debate the welfare system. I interacted with non-profit leaders who had various philosophies on why poverty exists and how to address it. I worked with volunteers eager to help the poor by giving a couple hours of their time each week. I also met committed Christians who had moved into poor neighborhoods and committed their lives to living among and sharing the struggles of their neighbors. Not surprisingly, this last group had an understanding of, and positive impact on, poor communities that far exceeded the others. All of this reinforced for me the importance of living among those God has called us to reach. In doing so, we imitate Christ who, as Eugene Peterson translated it so memorably, took on flesh "and moved into the neighborhood" (John 1:14, MSG).

During this time, I experienced a longing to go to seminary. I sensed that the time was drawing near for me to step forward into Christian leadership. Yet, my varied mission experiences were both teaching me many lessons and raising many questions. I was not always sure what the Bible or the Christian faith had to say about all this. The teaching I received in churches and in the Christian books I was reading seldom addressed these kinds of issues.

After three years in DC, during which time I met and married my wife Anne, we packed our belongings into a rental truck and drove across the country so I could attend seminary in Western Canada. We had no jobs lined up to support ourselves, but that was okay. We had both lived on missionary support before (Anne had been a missionary for two years in Africa). We knew God would take care of us.

Seminary afforded me a rich time to reflect theologically on my experiences in missions and poverty relief work. I learned the broad sweep of the biblical story and came to appreciate the theological themes that weave their way through. I began to see the big picture of how God is at work in the world and how my own efforts fit into God's larger purposes. One of the key theological discoveries I made along the way was the concept of the missional church. This theology was fairly new at the time but has since sparked a significant movement in Western Christianity. In essence, it asserts that God is on a mission to save the world and has called all of his people to participate in that mission.

Missional thinking contends that weekly worship attendance is not the gravitational center of the Christian life. Churches should not be organized so that everything revolves around the worship service. The goal of a congregation's outreach should not be to get people to attend church services. Further, the measure of someone's church commitment or spiritual health should not be determined by how often they are found sitting in the pew. Rather, missional thinking insists that biblical Christianity centers on participating in God's mission to redeem and restore God's creation through Jesus Christ. Thus, churches should organize themselves around involvement in that mission. Congregations should focus less on getting new people to attend their services and more on going to where people are and being present there. Christian commitment should be measured more in terms of missional engagement and less in terms of Sunday attendance.

At this point, let me offer three clarifications. First, missional theology is not actually new. Rather, it is a recovery of an ancient and original impulse and self-understanding which the church lost somewhere along the way. Christianity began not as an institution centered upon well-programmed Sunday gatherings but as a movement of spiritual extended families who worshipped the living Lord as they took his gospel wherever they went.

Second, in missional thinking, mission is not equated with missions. Traditionally understood, missions is something churches do when they send representatives (missionaries) to further God's work somewhere else, generally in a different culture. By contrast, mission (in missional understanding) is something God does, and it entails God sending the whole church on God's mission. Thus, churches not only send missionaries to faraway places; we are also sent by God as missionaries to our own communities and neighborhoods.

Third, a missional perspective does not necessarily hold that worship is less important than mission. Rather, it questions whether what happens in church services can be equated with what the Bible means by worship. Worship in its essence entails expressing our service, submission, and adoration to God. This involves much more than singing songs, celebrating the sacraments, or listening to sermons. Worship requires our whole lives, lived in pursuit of God's kingdom. Thus, a life lived on God's mission can be a life imbued with worship. Of course, there is plenty to celebrate, sing about, and learn from God's word along the way.

As a young seminarian, missional theology made sense of my Christian experience and my reading of the Bible. It also gave me a framework through which to understand and interpret my own missional journey. Yet, it would be sorely tested when I began my first pastorate.

Back in a local church after seminary, I found myself experiencing again the disconnect I had felt as a teenager and college student. It was almost as if what I had read about in the Bible and experienced in my twenties was somehow a different religion than what was being practiced in church. Of course, I quickly learned that the congregation I now served as pastor was not interested in changing religions! Let me explain.

As I got to know my new congregation, I came to realize that many of them had signed up to believe in a Jesus who would forgive their sins and secure them a place in heaven. In return, they expected to regularly attend Sunday services, to put something in the offering plate, and perhaps to volunteer to serve in a ministry, as time and interest allowed. They would also, of course, try to cultivate a personal relationship with Jesus, attempting to become better people, praying, and getting to know their Bibles. Many found great comfort and strength in their faith, and a few devoted a great deal of their lives to supporting the church or to following other callings into which they sensed God leading them. Occasionally, one or two would even become so committed to Christ that they, like I had, would volunteer to go off and serve as overseas missionaries. For most, however, the idea that they should devote their lives to living as missionaries right where they lived was not what they had signed up for.

As I took stock of my new church, I often wondered if I was being too hard on us. Plenty of good things were happening. Many in our congregation were growing in their faith. Some tried to share their faith with others when opportunities arose. We had several ministries which served our local community in addition to our support for cross-cultural missions. When I stepped back and looked at us, we were a solid Bible-believing, Jesus-centered church. Weren't we already serving as a beacon of light in our community, right where God had placed us? Certainly, we could always do better, but perhaps we were already missional after all.

Somehow, however, I could not shake my suspicion that the whole organization, culture, and purpose of our church and the lives our people were leading had too little to do with joining God in redeeming the world. When I looked at our church budget, we were spending so much of "God's money" on ourselves. So much of our time and energy went into our own building and fellowship activities. So many of our prayers focused on our own needs and concerns.

What is more, I had to admit that as pastor, I was spending almost every hour of my week with people who were already Christians. Of course, we did it all in the name of Christ and for the glory of God. Still, I had the uneasy feeling that we were missing the essence and the fullness of the Christian life. It felt as if after spending over a decade playing competitive football, I was now charged with overseeing a football fan club. This club watched games, swapped trivia and memorabilia, and for the especially faithful, played the occasional pick-up game in the lot out back. They assured me and one another that they were all about football. Yet, it seemed to me that I was spending far too much time organizing fan events and settling fan squabbles, and far too little time coaching a real football team.

Now in my late forties, I can stand back and see that a certain amount of the disconnect and discontent I felt toward the local church fifteen years earlier as a young pastor was due to my own youthful idealism. Young people are often passionate and idealistic, and I certainly was. I am also naturally a cause-driven person. What is more, until my thirties I had enjoyed freedom from family and financial responsibilities which allowed me to pursue my God-inspired dreams. Four children and countless diaper changes, sleepless nights, and soccer drop-offs later, things look different. Late-night "God talks" and intense prayer times with college buddies are a thing of the past. The financial calculus of investing my time and money in God's kingdom looks different now that college tuition bills are on the horizon. Churches, of course, are full of people wrestling through such adult concerns and responsibilities, while college fellowship groups are not.

However, age and season of life cannot fully explain the disconnect I felt. For one thing, my own experience as a pastor is not unique. It is almost proverbial among clergy that what led us into professional ministry in the first place was the joy and satisfaction of seeing Jesus transform people's lives. Yet, what we often experience is the unrelenting pressure of preparing sermons, attending meetings, organizing programs and volunteers, solving conflicts and problems, and meeting the needs of numerous congregants. Many a pastor has woken up on a Monday morning utterly drained and disillusioned and prayed, "Lord, how did I ever get here? I signed up to help people know Jesus better, and yet I find myself mostly just keeping a religious organization afloat."

What is more, young people today are leaving the church. While this phenomenon is not completely new, it used to be that when they got married and had children, they came back. Researchers are now telling us, though, that with the millennial generation (those born in the eighties and nineties) this is not the case. As my own experience illustrates, many young people do not find what they experience in church to be relevant or compelling. Of course, there may be some truth to the accusation that this new generation is simply too shallow and self-centered to want God. Yet, we must also seriously consider the possibility that many young people want more of God and God's grand purposes than the church seems able to offer them.

This book is a reflection on how so many churches today have gotten to this point. It is also a plea that we rediscover our missional identity and calling. I have now served as a pastor for fifteen years in two different congregations. Along the way, I have wrestled with how to lead these churches in becoming more missional. I have also had opportunities to advise a number of other churches in how to take steps in this direction. I am convinced that becoming missional will help us find our way back to the kind of alive and vibrant Christianity described in the Bible. In the next chapter, we will explore what the Bible has to say about being missional.

Questions for Discussion or Reflection

- What struck you from this chapter?
- Prior to picking up this book, what was your understanding of missional?

- In what ways does your church (or a church you used to attend) place "going to church" at the center of the Christian life? From what you know about Jesus's teaching, what does he place at the center?

- What might it look like to reorganize church or life around mission?

- Where in the past have you experienced compelling, vital, faith-stretching Christianity? What connection did that context have with mission (if any)?

- Do you know any young people who have left the church? Did they leave because the church offered them too much of God or not enough?

- What action will you take in response to what you learned in this chapter?

CHAPTER 2

God's Story

CONTEXT MATTERS. TAKE, FOR example, the familiar American phrase "separation of church and state." While these words are not actually in the U.S. Constitution, the general concept is there, and this phrase undoubtedly expresses an important aspect of what it means to be America. In recent decades, however, the phrase has become a source of conflict among Americans. Historically, faith communities invoked it in an effort to keep the government out of their business. Yet, during the past several decades, some civil liberties groups have returned the favor by using the phrase to argue for the removal of religious activities and displays from public life. In response, conservative Christians have countered that America was founded on the ideal of freedom *of* religion, not freedom *from* religion.

Who is right? Does "separation of church and state" mean that all religions (or all Judeo-Christian religions) should be equally welcomed into our public life? Or does it mean that all religions should be kept out of public life? If we want to know what our Founding Fathers meant by the phrase, we will have to go back and learn what the phrase meant in its original historical context.

The purpose of raising this thorny question is not to delve into politics. It is rather to remind us that context matters. Every statement is spoken in the context of a larger conversation. Every event occurs in the context of a broader history. When we take a statement or event out of its context, its meaning can become distorted or even reversed.

Unfortunately, Christians have too frequently been guilty of just such decontextualizing. We have often been content to memorize a few Bible verses or to rely on a short statement of theological beliefs, rather than to comprehend the broad sweep of the biblical story. This tendency is understandable. After all, how many of us have begun to read through the Bible in a year only to bail out halfway through Leviticus? Getting our minds around the entire biblical story can feel like a herculean task.

Yet, missional theology contends that much of what passes for biblical Christianity today fails to take the entire biblical story seriously. Far too often, Christians have selectively lifted favorite verses and doctrines out of the context of God's story. Then, unwittingly, we have reinterpreted these biblical nuggets in light of our own stories. In the process, our faith has become less about God and more about ourselves. In so doing, we have lost the big picture. We have forgotten that the biblical story is the story of God's passionate, undaunted mission to redeem the world. As a result, we have failed to appreciate that the gospel entails a summons to join God on this mission. With these claims in mind, let us take a walk through the biblical story.

Old Testament

In the beginning, God created a world which was good (Gen 1–2). Within this creation, humanity enjoyed dignity and purpose, peace and intimacy with one another, a symbiotic relationship with the earth and its creatures, and a rich and fulfilling relationship with their Creator. In particular, God tasked humanity with populating the earth and bringing order, meaning, and direction to what God had made (Gen 1:28). This creation mandate continues to be the privilege and responsibility of all people today. As we bear and raise children, we form families, communities, and nations, joining God in creating life and human community. Through science, agriculture, art, and many other kinds of work, we shape and bring out the potential in the raw materials God has provided us.

In the beginning, all that God created was in accordance with God's purpose and intention. Somewhere along the way, however, humanity decided to explore their ability to manage their lives apart from God and God's will (Gen 3). This fatal and rebellious choice drove a wedge between God and humanity and quickly led to the unraveling of all the harmonious relationships the creation had enjoyed. Still, even as God confronted humanity on their sinful decision, the LORD promised that he would one day defeat the forces of evil which were now unleashed in his creation (Gen 3:15). Against that backdrop, God's mission unfolds.

Almost four thousand years ago, the LORD revealed himself to a pagan Mesopotamian man whom we know as Abraham. The Bible tells us that a great building project had recently been abandoned in a city named Babel (also known as Babylon) (Gen 11:1–9). God had shut this project down because it epitomized all that was corrupt and wicked in the world. The city's prominent religious tower, in particular, embodied humankind's arrogant attempts to achieve greatness and self-sufficiency apart from God. In fact, the tower at Babel may have represented an effort to get heaven to support and bless humanity's godless agenda.[1] Yet, God's answer to this center of religious, cultural, and political power was not just judgment and rejection. On the contrary, God responded to Babel by recommitting himself to his mission to save his creation. The LORD began by going to the margins. There God called one man and his wife to walk with the LORD by faith, in vulnerability, weakness, and relative obscurity (Gen 12:1–3).

The LORD called Abraham and Sarah to leave their homeland and their people, everything dependable and familiar. In return, God offered an incredible promise. The LORD would bless them, and through them and their numerous descendants, God would bless all the nations of the earth. This call and this promise reverberate down through the entire story of the Bible. With them, the LORD bound himself to use one special people to accomplish his mission to redeem and restore his broken creation.

---

1. Ziggurats in the ancient world were constructed to provide the gods with stairways and accommodations for their visits to earth.

Fast-forward four or five hundred years. After a slow start, Abraham and Sarah's descendants have now grown and blossomed into a multitude of people. Still, the Israelites are living at the margins. The greatest nation on the earth is now Egypt, and like their forbearers at Babel, the Egyptians are arrogant and oppressive. In fact, they have conscripted Abraham's descendants into brutal slave labor (Exod 1). God is still committed to his mission, though, and with the birth of a man named Moses, God prepares to move that mission forward.

At a burning bush, the LORD calls Moses to go to Egypt's ruler and to demand that Pharaoh let God's people go (Exod 3–15). Moses reluctantly goes, and Pharaoh, not surprisingly, refuses to part with his slaves. So begins a mighty act of deliverance as the LORD brings ten plagues against Pharaoh and the Egyptians. The plagues culminate with a final act of redemption in which the LORD makes a distinction between his chosen people and the Egyptians. Jews remember it today as the Passover. The LORD instructs each Israelite family to slaughter a lamb at twilight. This substitute's blood will spare them from the deadly judgment the LORD will bring that night on the families of Pharaoh and the Egyptians. By the time this night of salvation and judgment is over, Moses is leading God's people out of bondage. When Pharaoh changes his mind and pursues them, God vanquishes the Egyptian army once and for all in the waters of the Red Sea. Yet, the LORD carries his own people safely through.

Redemption! God has set his people free. In the process, the LORD has revealed to Egypt his great power and his love for his chosen people. The LORD's reputation quickly spreads to the surrounding nations as well (Josh 2:8–11). Furthermore, an assortment of other peoples choose to leave Egypt with the Israelites and become part of God's people (Exod 12:38). As the biblical story continues, others from the nations will choose to be written into the story of God's mission as well. Canaanites like Rahab, Moabites like Ruth, and Hittites like Uriah are examples. The LORD's promise to Abraham to bless the nations through his people is coming to pass.

Having brought his people safely out of Egypt, the LORD's next task is to form them into a nation. This will not be easy, since they have known nothing but slavery and oppression for generations. God will need to provide them with a system of laws, justice, and governance.

The LORD begins by making a formal covenant treaty with his people at a mountain in Sinai (Exod 19–24). The LORD commits to be their God and to accept them as his people if they are willing to live under the moral and legal framework he will set out for them. The LORD assures them that by following his leadership, God's people will be a unique and holy people. They will be like a kingdom of priests, representing the LORD to the other nations of the earth (Exod 19:5–6). The LORD will also come and dwell among them, thereby showing them his favor and setting them apart as his own (Exod 33:15–16). The people gladly accept. Yet, they very quickly prove unable and unwilling to live according to God's ways (Exod 32). It soon becomes abundantly clear that while the LORD has graciously saved them from Egypt, they need to be somehow saved from themselves.

How will God's mission to bless the nations through his people ever succeed when his own people would rather go and adopt the corrupt and oppressive practices of these nations? The answer is not forthcoming, and this tension drives the biblical storyline forward. In the meantime, the LORD sets up a system of blood sacrifices through which the Israelite priests can secure forgiveness for the people's sins and offenses against God (Lev 1–7; 16).

Of course, no nation can flourish camped before a mountain or wandering about the Sinai wilderness. Therefore, the LORD directs Moses and then his assistant Joshua to lead the people into a land of their own (Num 10–27). Along the way, the LORD frets about how this people can ever remain faithful to him in the comfort and prosperity of this fruitful land (Deut 31:14–29). After all, they cannot even keep their spiritual focus in the distraction-free desert. Sure enough, in the land, the twelve tribes of Israel devolve into feuding, lawless factions (Judges).

Rather than give up on them, however, the LORD steps in again. God acquiesces to set a human king over them, to unify them and to rescue them from their enemies (1&2 Samuel). After Saul proves to be a false start, the LORD installs David on the throne over his people. While David is far from perfect, he is nevertheless a man after God's own heart. Under the LORD's direction, King David establishes and upholds God's good rule over Israel. In response, the LORD lavishly promises that David will never fail to have one of his descendants ruling over God's kingdom (2 Sam 7). Through this gracious covenant, the LORD recommits himself to working out his mission through his people.

Under the rule of David and then his son Solomon we get further glimpses of God's people becoming a blessing to the nations. The list of David's armed guard reads like a who's who from the surrounding nations (1 Sam 23:24–39). Solomon's God-given wisdom and splendor attract notice from Tyre all the way to Sheba (1 Kgs 5; 10). The Psalmists wax eloquent about the glories of a kingdom ruled by a king who honors the LORD, administers justice, protects the weak and vulnerable, and shows God's goodness to the nations (e.g., Ps 72).

Yet, the days of David and Solomon prove to be too good to endure. After Solomon, king follows king, some more wicked than others (1 Kgs 12; 2 Kgs 25). The LORD repeatedly sends prophets to warn the rulers and their people to turn back to God. The prophets condemn their hearers for turning to other gods besides the LORD. They rebuke them for oppressing the poor, the needy, and the vulnerable (Amos 8:4–6). This is not the way the LORD has shown his people to live! Again, instead of being a blessing to the other nations through their distinct righteousness, God's people are seeking to become just like these nations. The prophets warn that the LORD will not tolerate such unfaithfulness forever. At the same time, the prophets hold out hope. God will never abandon his mission altogether. The LORD will always preserve a remnant of his people who are faithful.

After God's people again and again ignore the LORD's pleas to repent, God eventually does bring judgment (2 Kgs 17; 25).

Through the empires of Assyria and then Babylon, the LORD dismantles the Davidic kingdom and removes Abraham's descendants from the land God had given them. So begins a new chapter in the story of God's people. Now, those who remain true to the LORD must learn to live out that faith in exile, among the great, godless empires of the earth. Amidst pressure to assimilate and compromise, godly Jews like Daniel remain faithful to the LORD (Dan 1–6). What is more, they succeed in showing their oppressors what their God is like. Some pagan rulers even join them in worshipping the true God. Even in the midst of the tragedy of exile, God's mission continues to be worked out through the few who remain faithful to him.

These stalwart believers draw encouragement from the prophets who continue to hold out hope. The prophets declare that the LORD has not abandoned his greater plan to preserve a people for himself and to bless the nations through that people. One day the LORD will send his Spirit to give his people new hearts and to move them to keep his commands (Ezek 36:24–27). Furthermore, the whole earth will eventually enjoy the renewal and restoration God will bring through the godly descendant of David whom the LORD will raise up. What is more, all the nations will share in this glorious future (Isa 2:1–5; 9:2–7; 11; 65:17–25).

When the Persian empire succeeds that of Babylon, hope soars among the Jews that the LORD is about to redeem his people. The Persian ruler Cyrus allows a number of Jews to return and rebuild the temple of Jerusalem (Ezra 1). Yet, despite the efforts of godly leaders like Ezra and Nehemiah, the people fail to put their wicked ways aside. No Davidic king emerges, and the returned exiles remain but a backwater province subservient to the Empire. In time, Greece replaces Persia. Then, Rome replaces Greece. The faithful continue to wait and long for the day when the LORD will bring to fulfillment his prophetic promises.

New Testament

Finally, during the days of the Roman emperor Caesar Augustus, the long-awaited Davidic king is born (Luke 1–4). He is not born into halls of power but to vulnerable, dislocated parents and poor shepherds. God's mission once more issues from the margins. Prophecies and signs surround Jesus's birth and early life. He is to be named Jesus, which means "The LORD saves." He is the Christ (which means "the one anointed [as king]"), the descendant of David who will restore God's kingdom. This child will bring forgiveness and salvation to God's people and pour out God's Spirit upon them. And so, heaven confirms that in Jesus Christ, the LORD's promises to Abraham, Moses, and David are finally being fulfilled.

When Jesus reaches thirty years of age, he chooses to be baptized to identify with God's people. At this moment, his Heavenly Father fills him with God's Spirit and affirms Jesus's identity as God's beloved Son. God has sent his own Son into the world to carry out his mission! Jesus responds by retreating to the wildness to fast and to experience the tests and temptations all of God's people go through. However, unlike the rest of humanity, Jesus withstands Satan's temptations. Jesus refused to use his power and privilege for selfish purposes. Now, he is ready to undertake the mission for which God has sent him.

Jesus then begins moving among God's people proclaiming the good news: "The time has come . . . The Kingdom of God has come near. Repent and believe the good news" (Mark 1:15). Jesus demonstrates the reality of this announcement as well. He forgives and welcomes sinners and outcasts back into God's family; he heals the sick; he sets free those plagued by evil spirits; he feeds the hungry; he even raises the dead. Through Jesus, God is putting his broken creation back together again.

As Jesus proceeds, he gathers disciples, inviting them to be with him and to join him in God's mission (Mark 3:13–19). Following Jesus involves learning to do what Jesus does and to live the ways of God's kingdom. In time, Jesus selects twelve of his followers to be his apostles, thus symbolically re-forming the twelve tribes of Israel. Jesus then sends these messengers out to share God's kingdom with others (Matt 10). To be chosen to lead in God's kingdom is to be chosen to go on God's mission.

While these stories may be familiar to us, they were not the way his contemporaries expected God's kingdom to be re-established on earth. Unlike his forbearers David and Moses, Jesus does not raise a military force to throw off his people's oppressors, nor does he set up a new governmental system based on God's law (John 6:15). Jesus's unusual methods baffle even his own disciples. Yet, perhaps they should have realized that the approaches they expected the Messiah to use had never been lasting in their effectiveness before. Moses's law had been only partially effective at gaining outward compliance among God's people. It had been far less successful in shaping the desires and inner motives of the human heart (Rom 7). If Jesus is going to set up an everlasting kingdom, God's Spirit must give its citizens new hearts as the prophets had foretold (John 3:1–15).

Jesus also teaches the people, renewing, re-contextualizing, deepening, and expanding the law Moses had given (Matt 5–7). Jesus makes clear that at the heart of obedience to God is justice, mercy, faithfulness, and especially, sincere and selfless love (Matt 22:34–40; 23:23). These are the character qualities which must typify those living in the upside-down kingdom Jesus has come to establish. Jesus also explains that not everyone will react positively to God's kingdom. Some will enter it with joy, but others will ignore or reject it (Mark 4:1–20).

While Jesus's own disciples struggled to come to grips with Jesus's very different way of bringing God's kingdom, his enemies grew more and more threatened and oppositional to his message and tactics (Mark 11–15). Jesus was undermining their sacred religious traditions and institutions, and this cut at the heart of their own honor, power, and privilege. Meanwhile, Jesus was setting himself up as Israel's authoritative teacher, and before all was said and done, he admitted that he was God's own promised king and divine Son (Mark 14:61–62). This was more than his opponents could stand. Therefore, after a mock trial, they crucified him in terrible shame and agony.

Yet, Jesus had anticipated his death. On the eve of his arrest, he celebrated a Passover meal with his disciples, predicting that he was about to lay down his life in love for the sins of many (Matt 26:17–30). As with the Passover lamb, Jesus's blood would shield from God's judgment those who placed their faith in him.

Jesus had also assured his disciples that on the third day after his death, he would rise again. And so it was that on the third morning his followers found the tomb empty (Luke 24). On that Sunday and in ensuing days, Jesus appeared bodily to many of them. His resurrection was the vindication and proof of all Jesus had done, claimed, and taught. It was also God's final defeat of death, so that now all who follow Christ can join him in eternal life (John 11:25–26). Meanwhile, Jesus told his disciples he must ascend and take his throne at God's right hand. From there he would pour out God's Spirit on all his followers. Through the Spirit, Jesus would continue to be with them and would empower them to participate in God's mission.

Finally, Jesus commissioned his followers, sending them to continue doing what he had done and to keep sharing the good news about him with others (Matt 28:16–20). Jesus made clear that being his disciples meant making disciples of others. He had not come and died for them alone. God was still committed to God's mission to bring the blessings promised to Abraham, which were now being fulfilled in Christ, to all the nations. As God had sent his Son on God's mission, so now the Son was sending his church (John 20:21).

And so, the Christian movement was born, a movement we still find ourselves part of today. After Christ poured out God's Spirit on his followers on the day we call Pentecost, their numbers began to grow and multiply (Acts). As they fanned out across the world of their day, they did the mighty deeds Jesus had done, shared the good news about Christ, and taught the ways of God's kingdom. They told how, by placing one's faith in Jesus, anyone could receive God's forgiveness, the gift of God's Spirit, and a new heart. They lived compelling and attractive lives of loving service and sacrifice. Wherever their message was accepted, the Jesus followers formed new communities of disciples. They taught these new churches to live the ways of Jesus.

At first, Jesus's followers took the message only to their fellow Jews. However, before long God's Spirit led some of them to share it among pagan peoples, too (Acts 10–15). When these non-Jews received it gladly, Jesus's followers had a decision to make. Could these pagan peoples be included in God's kingdom without first converting to Judaism? Years of prejudice against non-Jewish peoples created strong resistance to accepting them as they were. However, the guidance of the Spirit and the church's careful reflection on the implications of the gospel overcame this resistance. Walls of prejudice were torn down, and before long, the movement went forward equally to Abraham's descendants and to the other nations as well. Abraham's descendants had indeed become a blessing to the nations.

Today, God's mission continues on. Jesus has promised that once it has reached all nations, he will return and fully and finally establish God's eternal kingdom (Matt 24:14). At that time, God's people and the rest of creation will be fully renewed, restored, and transformed, while God's enemies are defeated and judged. So we will enjoy God forever and ever (Rev 21–22).

That is God's big story. Probably, few of the details I have shared are new to you. However, I hope you have been able to see in a fresh way the broad sweep of the biblical story. Ever since humanity spoiled God's creation, God has been on a mission to redeem and restore it. Missional thinking contends that we as the church must understand ourselves in light of this story. The story of God's mission graciously invites us to receive God's salvation. Yet, it also challenges us to share that salvation with others. The church exists because God loves us and chooses to include us in his story. The church also exists that we may further that story, bringing it to others. As Christopher J. H. Wright puts it, "If, in Christ, we inherit

Abraham's blessing we also inherit Abraham's mission."[2] Therefore, "It is not so much the case that God has a mission for his church in the world, as that God has a church for his mission in the world."[3]

This understanding of the Bible answers the age-old question of why God does not take us to heaven immediately when we "get saved." One reason is because God has saved us, in part, so that we can bring his salvation to others. God does not intend to save us from this world. Rather, God intends to save this world through us!

Another reason is because the "heaven" God has saved us for is not a misty, cloudy existence somewhere "up there." It is rather a renewed and transformed creation "down here" (Rom 8:20–21). Again, God does not intend to save us from this world. Rather, God intends to save this world for us. What I mean is this: while the Bible teaches that in some sense this present world will pass away (2 Pet 3:10), it also teaches that in some sense God will transform aspects of this world into something new, glorious, and eternal (Rev 21). How all this will work is certainly a mystery. Yet, God has told us enough to make clear that the church's calling until Christ returns is to join in God's mission to bring as much redemption and restoration to this world as we can. We do this not expecting that we can create a worldwide utopia, but that we can see God bring in and around us more of the healing, blessing, and goodness of the kingdom.

Missional theology describes our calling this way: God has sent the church as his *agents* to further God's mission in the world. We are also to be a visible and prophetic *sign* to the world that God is at work redeeming and restoring his creation, and all are invited to participate. Finally, by the way we live together, we are meant to offer the world a *taste* now of the New Creation which is coming.[4] Imagine if there were more Christian communities among whom a visitor could experience a taste of heaven.

2. Wright, *Mission of God's People*, 81.

3. Wright, *Mission of God's People*, 24.

4. Guder, *Missional Church*, 100–01.

In the next chapter, we will explore why the church is waking up to its missional calling and identity now.

Questions for Discussion or Reflection

- What struck you from this chapter?

- Describe a time when someone took a Bible verse out of context. What was the result?

- How well do you know the over-arching story line of the Bible? How would you summarize the biblical story in a few sentences?

- How often does the New Testament stress that we should "go to church?" What does it stress instead?

- From what you know of the New Testament, what did New Testament churches do together?

- To paraphrase Christopher J. H. Wright again, what is the difference between God's church having a mission and God's mission having a church?

- What action will you take in response to what you learned in this chapter?

CHAPTER 3

The Western Church's Story

IN 1974, LESSLIE NEWBIGIN retired after serving almost forty years as a missionary in India. Rather than catching a flight home to Britain, Newbigin and his wife Helen chose to travel across Asia over land. Bringing home only two suitcases and a backpack, they rode the bus most of the way, hitchhiking when necessary.

Back in Britain, Newbigin began to reacquaint himself with his home country. As he did, Newbigin came to a startling realization. In his absence, his own country had become a mission field. Some of the trappings of Christianity remained. Yet, Newbigin realized that, at its core, British culture had largely reverted to paganism. Of course, the gods of the British were no longer supernatural beings. They now worshipped the individual pursuit of power, wealth, and sexual experience. Likewise, they no longer turned to spiritual masters or traditions for truth and wisdom. Rather, they looked now to reason and science, or increasingly, they gave up on the search for truth altogether. As a result, when a Christian Englishman like Newbigin shared his beliefs with a friend, he was increasingly met with incomprehension and incredulity. The Christian message no longer resonated in British culture as being plausible or attractive. It no longer sounded like good news. The reason, Newbigin recognized, was that the church's message entailed many assumptions which British culture no longer found reasonable. It was no longer obvious to Brits, for example, that they were sinners in need of forgiveness, that the Christian God was real, that God had revealed himself through the Bible, or that Christ was more than a good man.

Newbigin began speaking and writing about his realizations. He urged the church not to respond to Britain's rising spiritual disinterest with passive resignation. He encouraged them instead to rediscover their calling as missionaries right in their own locale. You see, Newbigin had encountered a similar rejection of the Christian message in India. He had learned that this is to be expected on the mission field. The cultural presuppositions that underlaid Indian society were not Christian. Thus, when Newbigin had communicated the Christian message in India in the same way he had done in pre-war "Christian" England, the people of India had not found it plausible. Therefore, Newbigin had learned to do what missionaries routinely do. They study the local culture and work out how to contextualize the gospel in ways which can be received and understood by that culture. This is what Newbigin knew the British church now needed to do in its own country.

What was becoming true of Britain in the 1970s is now commonplace throughout the Western world. Christian culture is nearing extinction. It is being replaced by a reality many are calling post-Christendom. In a post-Christian world, the methods of communicating the Christian message on which churches used to rely are far less effective. Sharing the plan of salvation with a coworker or inviting a friend to church is no longer as likely to be met with a positive response. As the gap between the culture in our churches and the culture in the surrounding society has widened, a cross-cultural missionary approach has become necessary.

In the decades since Newbigin began speaking and writing about these challenges, the Western church has been waking up to our missional calling. That is, we have been coming to embrace our calling to be missionaries at home as well as to send missionaries abroad. Of course, this realization does not come easily. For centuries, Western countries have viewed ourselves as sending countries. We have understood our responsibility in world missions as being to send missionaries to far-off lands where the needs are greater. There is a subtle pride in this identity. It is a tough pill to swallow that other nations are now sending missionaries to us. Yet, a missional perspective challenges us to humble ourselves and to recognize the need for significant missionary work right here at home.

The Missionary Challenge at Home

Hopefully, this brief history lesson has helped answer the question "Why now?" If the biblical story is really the story of how a missionary God has sent his church to participate in God's mission, then why are we just now discovering this fact? Is missional thinking really biblical, or is it just the latest theological fad?

What I have hinted at in introducing this chapter is this: it sometimes takes a significant historical jolt for Christians to rediscover a major truth which is right there in the Bible. Anyone with at least a rudimentary knowledge of church history will recall other cases of this happening. For example, the Renaissance was critical in enabling Martin Luther to rediscover the doctrine of justification by faith and in sparking the Protestant Reformation. As the saying goes, Erasmus laid the egg that Luther hatched. Likewise, European colonialism brought an awareness of the "heathen world" to Europe which helped prompt the eighteenth-century Protestant rediscovery of the biblical mandate to take the gospel to the nations. Similarly, the epochal shift from Christendom to post-Christendom is causing the Western church to rediscover its missionary responsibility right at home. This rediscovery has helped us to realize that it is actually not biblical enough to say that God calls some to go as missionaries and the rest of us to stay home and support them. Rather, the biblical story insists that God has sent his whole church on God's mission. Wherever we are, we are God's missionaries there.

If we are going to understand the missional challenge before us in the West, we are going to have to do what Newbigin did. We are going to have to come to grips with the significant cultural changes taking place around us today. For the thousand-plus years that Christendom lasted, the church and the Christian religion held a privileged place in Western society. Christian presuppositions, thought categories, and values were deeply ingrained in

Western culture. In a Christendom context, the church could comfortably play the role of chaplain. It could serve as a moral compass and conscience for the culture. It could be present for families at important times like when babies were born, children were confirmed, couples were wed, and the dead were buried. At these and other moments, the church could seek to welcome people back to church and to reengage them in congregational life. Above all, it could help them to understand more clearly the way of salvation. All of these activities were within the realm of what was normal, acceptable, and believable within Western culture.

All of that is now rapidly changing. Certainly, Christendom has looked different at various times and places, and so the waning of Christendom looks different in various locations as well. For the purposes of illustration, therefore, let us just consider the differences that have taken place in mainstream American culture between the 1950s and today.

It is hard for young people today to appreciate just how "Christian" America still was in the middle of the twentieth century. In 1954, Congress added the words "under God" to the pledge of allegiance at the encouragement of President Dwight Eisenhower. Theologians like Reinhold Niebuhr were popular and well-respected American thought-leaders. The Catholic Archbishop Fulton Sheen starred in a popularly watched TV program on religion.[1] Church attendance was at an all-time high, with almost half of the American population telling pollsters on a given Sunday morning that they were in church. Many public schools began each morning with a Bible reading and the recitation of a short prayer. Christian clergy were respected members of society, regularly presiding over important civic events. Even Americans who did not consider themselves practicing Christians likely knew who Adam and Eve, Moses, and Jesus were. They also likely understood what sin was and took for granted that they would go to either heaven or hell when they died.

Contrast that with today. "Under God" is still in the pledge, but that is about where the similarities end. Pastors and theologians

---

1. Tickle, *Great Emergence*, 68–69.

are no longer trusted and respected voices in American society. In some cases, they are viewed with suspicion or even disdain. Church attendance is closer to one third and falling. Prayer in school has been outlawed. Few young people can answer even basic questions about the Bible or Christian beliefs. Many have never been inside a church building, except perhaps for a wedding or funeral. Today, society sends a strong message that people of faith should keep their beliefs private. Further, any belief which claims to be truer than other beliefs or seems exclusive, intolerant, or judgmental is strongly disapproved of. Thus, churches are increasingly viewed as out of touch or even bigoted and oppressive.

Nevertheless, many churches are continuing to function as they did in the 1950s, with very different results. When a Christian invites a friend to church, the friend is less likely to accept. After all, to them it is a foreign, irrelevant, or even threatening place. When Christian leaders speak up on moral issues, society is deeply suspicious that the church is seeking to impose its beliefs on them. When Christians present the plan of salvation, it is less likely to come across as intelligible or relevant since many today do not have a Christian conception of God, consider themselves to be sinners, or believe that there is a heaven or hell.

All of this suggests that when the average church member walks across the street to say hello to their non-Christian neighbor, they are crossing a huge cultural chasm. If they have not been equipped by their church for this cross-cultural missionary encounter, they are unlikely to represent or communicate the gospel in a way that will sound like good news. To further appreciate how different the world is today, let us briefly consider two aspects of contemporary Western society which are shaping how people view Christianity.

Postmodernity

When scholars refer to the prevailing perspective of the Western world in the centuries leading up to the mid-twentieth century, they often use the term "modernity." Modernity is associated with the assumption that through reason and science, human-kind can figure out all that is important to know about the universe. Modernity was profoundly optimistic about humanity's ability to discover truth and to apply that truth to conquering and overcoming the ills, threats, and problems of human existence. During the middle of the twentieth century, a profound questioning of modernity began.

Two horrific world wars and other human-caused tragedies were among the reasons that Westerners began to seriously reevaluate the merits of modernity. Thinkers began to ask whether the search for truth was really benefitting the whole world, or whether it was enabling the powerful to extend their privileged status at the expense of the rest. Thus, rather than look at the world through the lens of truth, postmodern thinkers began to look at it through the lens of power. What they saw made them increasingly skeptical and pessimistic about the modernist enterprise. Rather than seeing well-meaning thinkers pursuing truth wherever it led them, postmodernists saw the privileged and powerful constructing truth in ways which benefitted and justified their own interests. Rather than seeing modernity as a pursuit of the betterment of humanity, they came to see it as the efforts of powerful, wealthy European men to colonize and exploit the weak and marginalized. The narrative modernity told, then, was not the truth, but rather a powerful worldview constructed to oppress others.

For this and other reasons, postmodern thinkers became deeply skeptical of all truth claims and doubtful that absolute truth was even knowable. They increasingly saw all appeals to truth as efforts to seize power over others. By contrast, they maintained that each individual or group can have their own point of view, their own truth. Postmodern thinkers held that we should be slow to question the truth of others, so long as their beliefs are not causing anyone to be hurt or oppressed.

For many postmoderns, Christianity is implicated in the evils and failures of modernity. After all, Christianity makes strong and absolute truth claims. Further, for hundreds of years, Christianity was the dominant religion of those who held power.

The historical record shows that it was often the religion of colonialists and slave-holders and that it was used to hold others in subjugation and oppression.

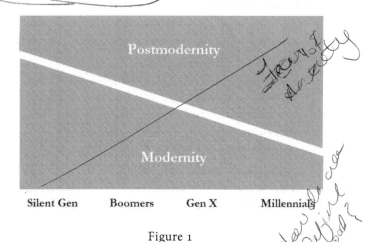

Figure 1

Obviously, postmodernity has a profound effect on the way people hear the gospel and on whether it sounds like good news to them. Of course, most people today do not have a fully postmodern perspective. We are living through the transition from modernity to postmodernity and so most of us have some combination of these two ways of thinking. As figure 1 illustrates, the Silent Generation (those born before the mid-1940s) tend to think more in modernist terms, while Millennials (those born in the 1980s and 1990s) tend to be largely postmodern in their thinking. This explains some of the reason why those who are younger are often ambivalent, suspicious, or down-right hostile to Christianity. They see it as a vestige of an old, failed, and oppressive worldview.

Red State Versus Blue State

The 2016 U.S. election and its aftermath have highlighted another growing dynamic in American culture: political polarization. Civil discourse has degraded into name-calling, demonization of political and ideological opponents, and an "echo chamber" in which people only consume the opinions and news (or fake news) which supports what they already believe. All of this has resulted in the widening of political divides and an increasing tendency to view those on the other side as immoral, as a threat, and as enemies. Meanwhile, the level of fear and anxiety in America continues to rise.

By and large, the church in America has taken sides in this conflict. Evangelicals have largely aligned themselves with conservative politics, while the traditional mainline denominations have primarily joined the liberals. In choosing to engage as combatants in the culture wars, the rival Christian camps have damaged their chances of representing God's kingdom in several ways. First, they have forfeited the opportunity to serve as reconcilers and peacemakers in the midst of the culture. Second, they have taken on the fear and anxiety of the culture rather than embodying and exhibiting a God-given peace which they might offer to others. Third, evangelicals, in particular, have effectively cut their mission field in half. By posturing themselves as enemies of liberalism they have alienated half the population. When the gospel comes from evangelicals' mouths, often accompanied by conservative viewpoints, those on the Left are far less likely to hear it as good news.

The Early Church

Missional thinkers have sought to address these and other missionary challenges. They have called the church to wake up and recognize the ways we have been taken captive by Western culture and its idolatries. They have called us to consider whether we are really "in the world but not of it" or whether we are actually "of the world and not in it." For example, in an effort to win the culture wars, have we inadvertently forfeited our witness and lost a hearing for the gospel? Have we put political and economic kingdoms before Christ's kingdom? Have we put our own individual happiness and prosperity before God's purposes and priorities? Have we prioritized our own individual stories over God's story and then

33

raided the biblical story for a few favorite verses we could use to spiritualize our individualism?

In calling the church to again find our proper place in God's purposes, the missional movement has pointed us back to our roots—to the early church. The early church began as a grassroots missional movement, largely powerless and persecuted. While living and engaging in the culture of their day, they refused to participate in its idolatries. They worshiped Christ as Lord and therefore refused to engage in the common cultural practice of confessing Caesar as Lord. For this and other reasons, they were persecuted and marginalized.

Despite having few religious buildings, paid staff, or other resources, early churches thrived. Meeting largely in homes, they functioned as extended spiritual families, supporting and caring for one another's needs, reaching out in love to their neighbors, and starting new communities wherever they went. In this way, the Jesus movement grew and spread until within three hundred years it had come to comprise half of the Roman empire, by some estimates.[2]

This astounding growth alone makes it obvious that the early church was extremely missional. Despite the fact that it was often illegal for Christians to publicly evangelize, churches were constantly adding new disciples to their ranks. The courage the Christians displayed in the face of persecution, the selfless compassion and care they showed one another and their pagan neighbors, and the miraculous power at work in and through them was so compelling that many wanted to know the Christ they followed. Yet, becoming a Christian was not a quick or easy process. For pagan seekers, it involved a demanding catechetical process of unlearning paganism, learning the teachings and ways of Christ, and testing whether one could embrace a life which often brought rejection, hardship, and even possibly execution. Only those who persevered through this process were baptized as Christians.[3]

---

2. E.g., Stark, *Rise of Christianity*, 10.

3. Kreider, *Change of Conversion*, 21–22.

All of this began to change in the years after Constantine came to power, as Christianity was increasingly welcomed into a privileged place in the Empire. Society began looking to the church for leadership, and converts flooded into the churches for many reasons, some of them less than spiritual. This new relationship between the church and culture led to many changes and adaptations within the church. Houses of worship were built, the size of congregations increased, and a class of professional clergy arose. Worship services were adapted to provide a basic knowledge of Christianity to the masses. The missional identity of the church faded, and missions came to be seen as efforts to extend the borders of Christendom in far-off, pagan places.

Whether these changes were all or even mostly bad has been hotly debated, and it is not the purpose of this book to weigh in on these matters. What is important to recognize is that while the Western church enjoyed this period of Constantinian Christendom up until the twentieth century, it is now rapidly coming to an end. What missional thinkers are seeking to wake us up to is the fact that the church can no longer go on functioning as we did when we enjoyed a privileged place at the center of a Christian culture. We must rather take our cue from the early church, realizing that at our heart we are a missional movement. That is not to say we should go back and do everything exactly the way they did it in the early church. After all, the culture we find ourselves in today is not pre-Christian, but rather post-Christian. Nevertheless, reacquainting ourselves with the story of the early church can shake us out of our Christendom assumptions and provide us with rich resources for the missional task before us.

Missional proponents are asking what it will look like for the church of Jesus Christ to have a missionary encounter with Western culture today. In seeking to answer this question, they have grappled with how the posture, mindset, structure, and activities of the church may need to change for this to happen. In the next chapter, we will begin to explore what being missional looks like in practice by dispelling some common misunderstandings of what missional is.

Questions for Discussion or Reflection

- What struck you from this chapter?

- List some ways Western culture has changed since the 1950s.

- What views and assumptions about the church are common in Western culture today? What are some ways the church can rebuild people's trust?

- What practices or assumptions used to serve the church well but no longer do?

- If engaging today's culture with the gospel is a cross-cultural endeavor, what skills and attitudes will we need to develop?

- Read Acts 13:13–43 and 17:16–34. Compare and contrast how the Apostle Paul contextualized the gospel for these two contexts (one Jewish, the other Greek).

- How good are you or your church at the missionary skill of contextualizing the gospel for the surrounding culture(s)?

- What action will you take in response to what you learned in this chapter?

CHAPTER 4

Missional Misconceptions

WHEN A NEW FAD arises, people copy it. Yet, not all of these imitations are the genuine article. When a new word becomes popular, lots of people start using it, but not everyone uses it properly. The word *missional* has certainly suffered this fate. Over the years, I have heard Christians voice many misconceptions about what missional is. Most of these people have it partly right but miss the heart and center of the matter. In this chapter, we will seek to sort out the facts from the fiction.

The word missional is quite simply the adjectival form of the noun mission. To be missional is to be sent on a mission, God's mission. To live missionally is, therefore, to live as a missionary sent by God to participate in God's mission. To be a missional church is to be a missionary community sent by God. In a sense, then, every Christian and every church is already missional whether we realize it or not. However, not every Christian and not every church are living out their missional identity and calling. How then do we know if we are truly missional? To begin answering this question, we will consider seven common misconceptions about what missional is.

Misconception #1: Missional just means
focusing more on outreach.

This is probably the most common misconception of what it means to be missional. Certainly, becoming more missional will result in more outreach, but it encompasses much more than that. Becoming missional involves more than adding outreach events to the church calendar. It involves more than starting new evangelism or service ministries. It involves more than going on more mission trips, whether locally or abroad. Becoming missional requires a wholesale conversion. It entails a recognition that our whole life is a missionary life, and our whole church has been sent by God on God's mission. This change in perspective is nothing short of revolutionary. It effects the way we look at everything. Becoming missional gives new meaning to the activities of our daily lives.

For example, when people are first learning about living missionally they often ask, "How am I going to find time to fit this into my life?" This question betrays an assumption that living missionally involves adding some missional activities to our current lives. Those asking it do not yet realize that many of life's activities are contexts in which to work out our calling as missionaries. For instance, a representative from a local internet provider stopped by our house one Saturday to offer us their latest deal. As I signed up (it was a good deal), she and I got into a great spiritual conversation. I wound up praying for her before she left. That day, living missionally took little extra time out of my schedule. It was simply an expression of how I was already living my life. Granted, as we come to view ourselves as missionaries, our priorities and time commitments will likely change. Our churches will likely devote more time, energy, and money to outreach efforts. But these are effects of becoming missional, not the essence of what being missional is.

Misconception #2: Missional means doing social action instead of evangelism.

At least two factors have caused a number of Christians today to downplay evangelism in favor of social action. One factor was mentioned in the last chapter. That is, the Christian message seems unreasonable or even offensive to a growing percentage of Westerners today. In response, some Christians have stopped speaking about their faith. Recognizing that those around them are suspicious of words, these Christians have contented themselves with demonstrating the gospel by the way they live their lives. A second factor involves the rediscovery that the gospel offers much more than salvation for individual souls after death. In the past few decades, many Christians have come to recognize that Christ's salvation encompasses the redemption and renewal of God's whole creation. This has spurred a renewed interest in Creation care, racial equality, social justice, etc., especially among younger Christians.

Both of these factors have prompted a number of Christians to pursue social causes or to live lifestyles of service, mercy, and justice. They have formed intentional communities in inner city neighborhoods, persuaded their small groups to serve monthly at soup kitchens, or recruited their friends to fight against human trafficking. Some have used missional as a label for these lifestyles and actions. In some cases, this may be because missional theology has highlighted the two factors mentioned above.

Missional thinking certainly affirms the importance of service and social action. After all, God's people are to live in the world as a prophetic sign and foretaste of what the world will be like when God's kingdom fully comes. When God's mission is complete, the hungry will be fed, the suffering will be comforted, the oppressed will receive justice, and those in bondage will be set free.

Nevertheless, being missional is bigger than social action for at least two reasons. First, missional living involves all of life, not just the hours we dedicate to service and action. For example, a man who attends my church was recently stuck in Binghamton, New York, due to inclement weather. As he walked through the downtown looking for a place to have dinner, he passed a young homeless man. After he walked past, he sensed God nudging him to go back and invite the young man to join him for dinner. He did so, and the two enjoyed a conversation over pizza which impacted them both significantly. While this man does not regularly serve among the poor, his understanding of himself as a missionary led him into such ministry at that moment. Likewise, a conversation in the checkout line while buying groceries can be as missional as the hours we spend volunteering with an environmental group. The time a church board or small group Bible study takes to work out their conflicts peacefully can be as missional as the time we take fixing up an old car for a single mom. Imagine if churches got the reputation of being communities who solve their conflicts graciously! Jesus said the world will know we are his disciples if we love one another (John 13:35).

Second, missional thinking does not downplay the importance of speaking about Jesus using words. On the contrary, missionaries must be prepared to explain how our actions embody or point to God's kingdom. We have been given good news to share—while our efforts may provide a taste of what life in God's kingdom is like, people can experience that goodness for themselves only through Jesus Christ. We must trust and follow Jesus to be reconciled to God and to continue enjoying the love, peace, healing, freedom, and justice of God's kingdom. Thus, being missional involves both showing and telling the good news.

Misconception #3: Missional is against foreign missions.

When we seek to make a correction, there is always the danger that we will over-correct. Some missional devotees have no doubt done so. In their eagerness to help us rediscover our missional calling at home, they have sometimes unintentionally downplayed the importance of missions abroad. In reality, missional theology embraces both locations for mission. God calls some of us to join God's mission in other places where the needs are greater than they are at home. Those who stay home must help fund and support those who go. Yet, missional theology reminds those of us at home that we are never merely senders or supporters. Rather, we are just as much missionaries right where we are. God has sent us all on God's mission.

Misconception #4: Missional is against programs.

Missional proponents have sometimes been perceived as being critical of church programs. For one thing, they talk a lot (as I have just done) about mission being a lifestyle, rather than a program or activity. Missional proponents also frequently point out that church programs require a lot of volunteers. As a result, programs keep countless Christians busy at church, leaving them precious little time to spend with those outside the church.

For these and other reasons, missional proponents tend to push church cultures toward becoming more organic and less organized. For instance, churches seeking to become missional frequently start missional communities. These organic expressions of church life are generally comprised of fifteen to forty people who regularly pursue spiritual growth together, eat and play, and participate in a common mission. Since time, money, and resources are always limited, churches which emphasize such organic approaches to mission often find it necessary to cut back on church programs.

However, missional theology does not teach that organic expressions of church are inherently superior to organized ones. What it does insist is that churches consider which expressions will allow them to develop a more effective missionary presence in their communities. Many churches have found that they must become more organic for this to happen. However, when a church can best fulfill its missional calling through programmatic means, it should be all means do so. There are certainly missional churches using programs very effectively.

Misconception #5: Missional is against attractional churches.

Because missional proponents frequently talk about the importance of incarnational ministry, they have often been perceived as being against attractional churches. Some of them certainly are.

However, I agree with others who believe that being missional is not necessarily antithetical to being attractional. Before I explain why, an explanation of terms might be helpful.

Attractional churches place an emphasis on getting people to come to their worship services and other programs. Like the woman at the well in John 4, they invite people to come and see who Jesus is. In the Old Testament, the Israelites were to fulfill God's mission in an attraction manner by being a holy people who would draw the nations to the LORD (Isa 2:1–5).

By contrast, an incarnational approach patterns itself after the Incarnation. The Son of God came to humanity and lived among us. Following Christ's example, an incarnational approach emphasizes the creating of new, contextual expressions of church among the people we are seeking to reach. It is a go-to-them, rather than a come-and-see approach. In the New Testament, we see the church living out this approach to mission as they take the gospel from Jerusalem and Judea to Samaria and the ends of the earth (Acts 1:8).

Two missional efforts led by members of my church may be helpful to illustrate these two approaches. In 2012, Hurricane Sandy slammed into the neighborhood where our church building is located, knocking out power for days. About this time, a group of church members were gaining a vision to use our building's coffeehouse space for outreach. Seizing the opportunity afforded by the hurricane, they fired up the church's generator and went door-to-door inviting neighbors into the café to charge their cell phones and to enjoy hot soup, board games, and conversation. One woman started attending our church as a result. This group then began seeking other ways to attract people to the café. For a while, they hosted weekly discussions on contemporary issues. Then, they tried offering free weekly guitar lessons. After that, they hosted a monthly open mic night. Finally, they showed popular movies followed by discussions on the spiritual themes in those movies. Some of these efforts led to spiritual conversations with participants who do not normally attend church. Recently, the group realized that they will be more effective in mission if they can focus on seeking to reach a particular group of people. They are praying that God will show them who this should be. This group is an example of an attractional approach to mission.

Several years ago, another couple in our church developed a vision to reach out to the square-dancing club to which they belong. They invited several other church members to join them. They started cooking soup for dances and making an extra effort to welcome newcomers who joined the club. They listened to people share their problems and offered to pray for them when it seemed appropriate. They went out of their way to offer support, counsel, and practical help when they could. When someone in the club died, they helped organize and conduct the funeral. This informal leadership began shaping the culture of this club, making it warm, caring, and inviting. Relationships deepened. When two couples expressed spiritual interest, two church couples in the club started meeting with them to explore who Jesus is using the Gospel of Mark. The goal of this missional effort is not necessarily to get anyone to attend our church but rather to see what sort of "church" might emerge right in the midst of the club. This is an example of an incarnational approach to mission.

The missional movement has definitely sought to recover and champion the incarnational approach. However, this is not because the attractional approach cannot be missional. It is rather because as Western culture becomes increasingly post-Christian, incarnational approaches tend to be far more effective. Let me explain why.

Every time a churchgoer reaches out to a person who is not a Christian, a cross-cultural encounter takes place. This is because church culture represents one culture and the surrounding culture represents another. When a Christian seeks to introduce someone else to their faith or their church, they are seeking to bridge these two cultures.

An attractional approach works well when the distance between church culture and the surrounding culture is narrow, as it was during the age of Christendom when society was culturally Christian. In that case, the church culture was not very foreign or threatening for the person being invited in. They could comfortably come and see, taste and explore.

In post-Christian contexts, however, the distance between church culture and the surrounding culture is great. What happens when this same attractional approach is used in such contexts? Now we are asking a person to leave their own familiar culture and to visit a culture which for them is foreign and perhaps threatening. They are unlikely to be comfortable or eager to take this trip and may not understand or appreciate what happens at church if they do. Also, isn't it inhospitable and even selfish of us to expect them to take this journey? Doesn't the love of Christ compel us, rather, to leave the comfort of our culture to meet others in theirs? Therefore, being missional often requires an incarnational approach. We must go to others to build trust, connectedness, and understanding. We must figure out ways to be the church among them so that they can taste and see the goodness of Jesus and his reign. We must not content ourselves with reaching the shrinking portion of the population who are still comfortable coming to church, while forgetting the growing percentage who will never come.

Yet, as important as incarnational approaches are becoming today, they are not the same thing as being missional. Attractional churches can also be missional in contexts where the surrounding culture is still fairly Christian. Thus, again, it is context which must determine what shape being missional takes.

Misconception #6: Missional is not for introverts.

There is a man in my church who seems to have a new story every couple of weeks about someone he told about Jesus, prayed for, or helped in some practical way. Some people in my church hear his stories and respond, "I could never do that. I'm not nearly as friendly and outgoing as he is." It is true that this man is a high extrovert who easily strikes up conversations with complete strangers. However, this does not mean introverts cannot be missional.

I am a fairly high introvert myself. I know firsthand the pressure and guilt I can feel when I compare myself to someone like our extroverted friend. Yet, I have also learned to find my own missional style which allows me to be myself while at the same time being attentive to what God is doing in the people around me. I have learned, for instance, that when I go to the grocery store or the coffee shop, I do not have to be constantly alert for a chance to interact with the people around me. I can retreat inside my introverted shell and block out the surrounding world. Yet, once I reach the checkout or deli line, this is the moment I need to step out of my comfort zone, to notice the people in line with me as well as the store clerk, and to be open, present, and friendly. Depending on the headspace those around me are in, no interaction may take place, we may exchange pleasantries, or on occasion, we may have a meaningful interaction.

I have also learned that doing mission as part of a team allows me to rely on the strengths of the extroverts in the group while I contribute what God has uniquely gifted me to do. For example, a friend and I regularly go to a local eatery. He is highly relational and has gotten to know the owner, the staff, and all of the regulars. He has even had several of them over to his house for dinner. Through him, I am slowly getting to know these people as well. Because I am good at listening, a couple of them have opened up to me in ways they have not to my friend. When one of them had spiritual questions, he specifically sought me out for my input. The combination of working as a team and predictably showing up at the same place again and again has enabled me to engage in mission in ways I could not by myself. Introverts may find mission more challenging at first, but we can certainly play an important and powerful role.

Misconception #7: Missional is not for ordinary Christians.

Few Christians today think of ourselves as missionaries. Many of us have not been trained to share the gospel, let alone to contextualize it for a different culture. Perhaps we tried to share our faith at one point, but it was an uncomfortable experience. Besides, our lives are already full trying to put food on our tables, to de-stress after a hard day at school or work, and to manage our relationships. Thinking about being a missionary feels overwhelming. Why not let the paid professionals at church worry about it? We will support them by volunteering for the programs they organize or occasionally inviting a friend to church. If our church needs to become more missional, we will let them figure out what that means. We will do our part by being supportive of their efforts.

The fact is that the churchgoing life just described is simply not the kind of life Jesus envisioned for his followers. Nor is it a life which aligns with the biblical story described in chapter 2. Certainly, plenty of churches, shaped by the consumer culture of the West, have allowed or even enabled this sort of life. Rather than training up spiritual producers, as Jesus expects his followers to be, these churches have contented themselves with attracting spiritual consumers.[1] They have built large religious organizations by doing a better job than other churches at serving the needs and catering to the expectations of Christians. While there are numerous problems with this approach, one is becoming increasingly clear. The world is looking at these religious institutions and saying "Who cares?" Particularly in post-Christian contexts, many large, well-run churches are quickly becoming irrelevant to the people around them. They are not fulfilling God's mission.

Here is where ordinary people come in. Churches cannot get back on track without them. If churches have any hope of becoming missional, it will be because the people in the pew take up their missional calling.

The New Testament makes it clear that participating in God's mission is the right, privilege, and expectation of every follower of Jesus. It is true that in Matthew's Gospel, Christ gives his famous Great Commission to a select group of apostles. However, Jesus had many more disciples besides these Twelve, and in Luke and John, it is this larger group of ordinary disciples whom Jesus

---

1. Breen, *Discipling Culture*, 17.

sends to be his missionaries. In John's Gospel, for instance, Jesus tells a group of "disciples" that as the Father has sent him, so he is sending them (John 20:21). John uses the phrase "the Twelve" when he wants to specify only the apostles (John 20:24), so here Jesus is sending his ordinary followers. Likewise, in Luke 24, Jesus commissions a room full of apostles and other followers for his mission (Luke 24:33). When we get to the book of Acts, we see other followers of Jesus joining the apostles in spreading the good news about Jesus. Even in Matthew, Jesus tells his apostles to teach the disciples they make everything Jesus commanded them. Thus, part of what every disciple is to be taught is the command to make disciples! In other words, to be a disciple is to make disciples. To be a follower of Jesus is to participate in God's mission. As the great preacher Charles Spurgeon once put it to his congregation, "Everyone here is either a missionary or an impostor."[2]

It is also worth pointing out that the Bible knows no distinction between a believer and a disciple. Contrary to what is sometimes assumed, discipleship is not a higher and more demanding level to which Christians graduate if or when they become super committed. In the New Testament, to believe in Jesus is to follow him, and if you are not willing to follow, you do not really believe. It is that simple. This is why the apostle Paul says in Ephesians 4 that God expects the church to equip all of God's people to do works of ministry (Eph 4:11-12). God's mission is so big that all of his people must participate if it is to be fulfilled. God has given each believer a different gift, and all of these gifts are necessary.

One of the great joys of being part of a missional church is seeing all the gifts working together. It is also a relief that not everyone has to be great at evangelism. In my twenties, I was part of a missional community that reached out to high school students. Several participants were teachers and would invite students along to our gatherings. One participant hosted us in her apartment and made sure everyone felt comfortable and had plenty of good food. Three other participants were great musicians and kept us entertained with songs, some of which they wrote themselves. A couple

2. Spurgeon, "Sermon and Reminiscence," § III.

others were gifted Bible teachers and would take turns presenting a short devotional. None of us had to do it all. Together, we formed a warm, inviting, attractive community which teens loved to be a part of. Several of the students who joined us regularly came to follow Jesus along the way.

This is the missional church in action. It is God's people embodying the love of Christ together and making it available and accessible to others. This is not something that the clergy can do for us or that church leaders must decide or organize. It is, rather, the people of God learning to be God's missionaries right where we are. In the next chapter, let's consider some of the characteristics missional churches possess.

Questions for Discussion or Reflection

- What struck you from this chapter?

- How has this chapter changed your understanding of what it means to be missional?

- In what ways is becoming missional bigger than just doing more outreach?

- Where you live and work, how wide is the gap between the surrounding culture and the culture in the church? What barriers keep people from coming to church?

- Is the approach of your church (or a church you used to attend) more attractional or incarnational? How appropriate is this approach for the size of the gap you described in response to the previous question?

- What hesitations do you have about viewing yourself as a missionary? What attracts you to the idea?

- Have you been discipled? Why or why not? If you were, did that discipleship equip you be a missionary in today's culture?

- What action will you take in response to what you learned in this chapter?

CHAPTER 5

Missional Characteristics

How is a missional church different from any other church? How is a missional life different from the typical Christian life? Let's look at seven characteristics those who are missional possess.

Missional attitude

Every congregation has longtime, faithful members who are pillars of the church. Year after year, they give generously, serve on committees, maintain the building, and volunteer for jobs no one else wants to do. Often, they serve with little thanks or recognition. Such people should be celebrated. Yet, they are also susceptible to a unique spiritual danger. The ownership they feel for their church too often devolves into a sense of entitlement. Their years of faithful service and sacrifice can leave them feeling that the church to which they belong is *their* church. They can begin to assume that they should have a significant say in how their church works. As they age, they can come to expect that their church will be there to provide for their needs for fellowship and social life and for support and pastoral care through sickness and old age. They may imagine that one day their church will conduct their funeral.

This attitude is understandable. After all, these people have paid their dues. They have remained committed when many others have come and gone. They have repeatedly stepped up when everyone else failed to do so. Often, they have a deep appreciation for how church should function as family. Yet, this attitude is also dangerous. It is dangerous because it fails to recognize that every church belongs to Jesus Christ alone. It is dangerous because it fails to appreciate that not a single one of us has earned the right to be a part of our church. Each of us belongs for only one reason—because Jesus Christ has invited us to be his guest. We each belong due to a sheer act of grace!

A missional attitude is rooted in an appreciation of this grace. A missional attitude recognizes that Christ has given and sacrificed infinitely more for us and our church than any of us ever will. A missional attitude realizes that we are part of God's family only because Jesus left his own place of comfort to face danger, suffering, and death so that we could be saved. A missional attitude involves a growing willingness to follow Christ's example by doing the same for others. Rather than receiving God's grace and hoarding it for ourselves, a missional attitude is eager to pass that grace along to others. In fact, anyone who does not want to share grace with others has not yet fully understood it! To have a missional attitude is to recognize that God went on mission to reach us, and now God has called us to join in that mission to reach others. Thus, my church and your church do not exist for our comfort or security. They exist for God's mission and purposes.

When we understand God's incredible grace for us and that God is catching us up in his grand purposes to share that grace with others, we are forced to confront our fears. Many churches have retreated from God's mission because they are afraid. They are afraid that the world around them will taint or corrupt them or their children. They are afraid that they are not good at mission, and they will fail. They are afraid that the culture will reject or even persecute them.

In my experience, one major reason people shrink back from mission is fear of evangelizing. One cause of this fear is the unavoidable reality that some folks find Christ offensive. Yet, another common cause is entirely avoidable. It stems from the fact that many Christians have been taught a method for sharing their faith that felt awkward to them and to those on whom they tried it out. The approach did not feel natural or authentic. The message they shared did not feel like good news. The whole thing felt canned, forced, or like they were supposed to treat the other person like a project.

I have experienced this sort of evangelism training myself. I once attended an evangelism workshop that encouraged us to ask strangers what their names meant. If their name had any spiritual significance, we were instructed to use this fact to transition into the gospel presentation we had memorized. Another session I attended trained us to ask people on the street to stop and answer a few survey questions. Our real goal, we were told, was to use their answers as an excuse to share the gospel with them. A third session on relational evangelism encouraged us to prayerfully select two friends to make into our evangelism projects. While such approaches may fit the personalities and inclinations of some Christians, many others find them to be unnatural or disingenuous.

I have found that Christians who have had such evangelism experiences often need to come to two realizations before they will engage in mission. First, they need to learn a new and different way to share their faith. I once led a group at our church called "Evangelists Anonymous." Its purpose was to help participants unlearn, detox, and heal from their past evangelism training. In its place, I sought to help them discover a very different way of sharing their faith, a more natural way, which is more honoring to the people to whom they are speaking. Thankfully, such approaches exist, and they are vital if we are to become missional.

Second, fearful Christians need to recognize that mission is more than evangelism. It involves service, working for justice, impacting culture, and befriending and welcoming people into warm, supportive community. When a church does mission together, not everyone has to be a great evangelist. Those who are more comfortable sharing their faith can take on a larger share of that responsibility. When we can overcome our fears and relax, mission becomes fun, energizing, and fulfilling.

Figure 2

Missional orientation

Many local churches view themselves like figure 2 above. They perceive themselves, along with other churches, to be the locus and center of what God is doing in their community. Their emphasis is often on their building and what takes place within it, particularly their worship services. When making decisions, they tend to do what is best for those already in their church, rather than for those on the outside. They frequently equate ministry with volunteering in the recognized programs and services of the church.

The mission of such churches is typically to worship God, to build up their people spiritually, to provide a warm, loving space protected from the influences of the world, and to bring new people to Jesus and into their church (represented by the arrows in the figure). In some cases, these churches do not distinguish between those they attract from other churches and those who are finding Jesus for the first time. The goal of such churches is often to increase their attendance, budget, and perhaps the size and quality of their building. To the extent that they accomplish these goals,

they may consider themselves to be succeeding in fulfil
mission and responsibility to Christ. They may speak of
"building God's kingdom" (a phrase never found in the E

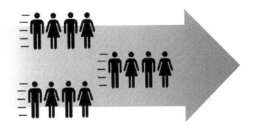

Figure 3

Missional churches have a different orientation. A missional
orientation recognizes that the locus and center of what God is
doing in a community cannot be equated with any local church.
God's work is bigger than the visible church and is taking place
both within and beyond it. Thus, missional churches orient themselves toward the kingdom of God which God is bringing near in
their communities (the large arrow in figure 3). Rather than thinking they can build God's kingdom, they aspire to discern, seek,
and participate in it. Missional churches therefore perceive themselves to be on the move, following God's leading in, through, and
around them. Their goal is to see God's mission be accomplished
in their communities as well as in their congregations.

Missional churches conceive of their mission not in terms
of *what* they are doing for God, but in terms of *who* God is calling them to reach. Most often, this "who" will be a neighborhood
or a network of people who have something in common. Today,
Western culture is fragmenting into an ever-increasing number of
tribalized sub-cultures. There are the single moms and the soccer moms, the skateboarders and the snowboarders, the slow food
meet-ups and the crowd at the soul food hangouts, the muscle car
enthusiasts and the microhouse owners, the recovery group regulars and the red-light prostitutes. On and on it goes.

Missional churches seek to follow God into these mission fields to represent, embody, and further God's kingdom there. The goal of this mission work is to see people personally redeemed and transformed by Christ, but it is also to see the whole community with its relationships, systems, structures, and even physical locations be redeemed and transformed as well. After all, Jesus taught us that this is what happens when the kingdom of God comes. Everything on earth starts to look more like it will in heaven (Matt 6:10).

In my twenties, I worked for a non-profit organization in our nation's capital. I soon learned that the old saying about Potomac Fever is true. People who move to Washington quickly get caught up in a culture focused on using others to get ahead. I witnessed my coworkers being quick to take credit for the successes of others and quick to blame others for their own failures. Several other Christians at my new workplace and I realized that this was not how Jesus had taught us to treat people. We staged a silent revolution, making a point to praise our coworkers and their accomplishments to our supervisors and to take responsibility for our role in any failures.

Over time, this approach began to change the culture of our organization. Respect, trust, and camaraderie grew. Our staff began to feel like a family in the midst of a dog-eat-dog culture. Through our witness, some of them wanted to know more about the Jesus we followed, but that was not the only reason for our little revolution. We recognized that God had placed us at this organization to reflect and further God's kingdom there, and where God is king, people take care of each other and loving community flourishes.

At the same time, a missional orientation definitely expects to see individual lives be transformed by the gospel of Jesus Christ. When people do begin a relationship with Jesus, missional churches avoid pulling these people out of their social circles and into the circle of the church. After all, how many churchgoers have mused that when they became a Christian, they got so busy with church activities that they lost all their old friends. Missional churches recognize that if a new believer is extracted from their previous social circle, the potential for God's kingdom influence in that circle is diminished just when the door has opened for it to expand!

Therefore, when someone begins a relationship with Jesus, missional churches go to be present with that person in their current life. They equip, disciple, and partner with new Christians to bring the presence and witness of God's kingdom to their existing social circles. In this way, missional churches seek out and participate in God's kingdom as it expands into the many subcultures of our world. This is the orientation of the missional church. It is not about building our own religious empire or protecting our church family from the influence of the world. It is about moving out into our community to see God's kingdom come there. This different posture leads to a different understanding of belonging and a different measure of success.

Missional belonging

Many churches conceive of belonging by drawing a boundary between those who are in and those who are out. They often have a membership list which clearly differentiates those who belong to the church from those who do not. While formal membership lists are not found in the New Testament, they have certain practical benefits. They delineate who is eligible to serve in leadership positions and who can vote on matters of church business. Yet, everyone who has spent much time around churches knows that church membership is a very imperfect measure of belonging. In most churches, you will find some strongly committed Christians who are not members, for various reasons. Most also have some voting members who are barely involved in the church or whose lives show little evidence of a genuine Christian commitment.

Because missional churches are oriented toward God's mission, their understanding of belonging will relate to direction rather than to boundaries. The life of Jesus illustrates what this looks like. Jesus came bringing God's kingdom, and a group of disciples gathered around him and followed him. As they explored together what life in God's kingdom entailed, some continued to follow, and others turned back. The question each faced was whether they were going to continue moving toward Jesus and his purposes or away from them. Trying to distinguish who was "in" from who was "out" at any given moment in the gospel stories only leads to frustration and disagreement. This is because the gospel writers were not addressing the question of boundaries. They were addressing the missional question of direction. This is not to deny that there is a moment in time when someone crosses the line of faith; it is only to recognize that we do not always know when that moment occurs. Furthermore, even when someone is converted, plenty of growth and transformation still needs to take place in their lives. We are all still very much on a journey.

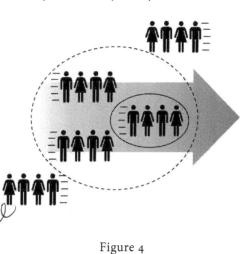

Figure 4

The question missional churches will ask, then, is who is travelling with our church in the direction of God's mission (dashed oval in figure 4)?[1] It is those who are moving toward God's kingdom who belong. Those who are moving away, choosing to distance themselves from Jesus and his purposes, do not belong. One missional church I know reflects this missional view of belonging in how they measure their attendance. In addition to counting how many show up at their worship services, they also add in how many people have regular (at least twice-a-month) social contact

moving toward His purpose

1. The use of dashed ovals to signify "centered sets" and solid ovals to signify "bounded sets" is borrowed from Guder, *Missional Church*, 206–14.

with their church community. For this church, the larger oval represents all those who are traveling with them on the journey of getting to know Jesus.

Yet, missional churches need not completely abandon boundaries. For many, believer's baptism sets an obvious boundary between those who have committed to a life of faith in Jesus and those who have not. Many also use boundaries in a limited way, to distinguish who the leaders or core group of the church are (solid oval in figure 4). What sets this smaller group apart is the high level of commitment they have pledged to the mission God has for that church. One missional church I know does not offer church membership but designates those who commit a high degree of support to the church's mission as "mission partners."

Missional measurement

All churches measure their effectiveness. Some do so intentionally, others unconsciously. Most churches measure the ABCs: attendance, buildings, and cash. "How big is your church?" is a common question. It usually means, "How many people typically attend your worship services?" Even churches that do not formally track their attendance will hear attenders say, "Boy, the service was really kind of empty this morning." People are counting. Yet, the number of people gathered in a room tells us little about whether a church is succeeding at what Jesus has called us to do. Jesus did not call us to build churches. He said he would do that. What Jesus called us to do is to make disciples. As Willow Creek Community Church discovered in their famous REVEAL study, whether people show up for a religious program is not a good measure of whether they are growing spiritually.[2]

Take a shoe factory as an example.[3] What is the most important measure of whether a shoe factory is fulfilling its mission? The answer is obviously how many pairs of shoes the factory is produc-

2. Hawkins and Parkinson, *Reveal.*
3. I once heard Randy Frazee use this analogy in a seminar.

ing. Presumably, the factory will measure many other things. It will likely measure how much pollution the factory is emitting, what percentage of materials are being.wasted, and how satisfied the workers are with their jobs. Yet, a factory could be receiving high marks on all these measures, and if it is not making any shoes, we would consider it a failure! The same is true for churches. A church may enjoy high attendance at its services and other programs, have a growing budget, and possess a spacious and beautiful building, but if it is not making more and better disciples, it is not fulfilling its mission.

What then will missional churches measure? The mission Jesus gave the church is to make disciples who look and live like Jesus. That is, the church is to raise up communities of people who together have the character, convictions, and competencies necessary to represent, embody, and further God's kingdom. Granted, these are challenging measures to quantify. How do we judge which church attenders are truly disciples and whether they are becoming better ones? Can we quantify how well a church is representing God's kingdom?

Nevertheless, measurement is necessary because what we count sends an often unintentional but powerful message about what is important. People instinctively want to know how to succeed and are motivated by what is being measured. Going back to our shoe factory analogy, if a factory measures how many pairs of shoes it is producing, managers will be motivated to lead differently than if it measures how satisfied workers are with their jobs. Likewise, if baseball officials counted how many hits players got rather than how many runs they scored, teams would play the game differently. Likewise, what a church measures tells its people what is important to that church and how that church can win.

Here is what some missional churches are measuring. Some are counting the mission-related stories being told in their congregations. These stories may be about an opportunity a church person had to bake cookies for a new neighbor or to pray for a coworker. Our church tells these sorts of stories in our worship services. We also tell "transformation stories" about how God is changing our characters and relationships to be more like those of Jesus. Other churches are measuring multiplication. For instance, in our church, I have discipled a group of leaders in how to live missionally and to disciple others. We are now counting how many of them turn around and do the same for others. Other churches are counting how many missional communities they have started and how many of those are multiplying into additional communities. Still other churches are measuring community impact. They are counting how many underprivileged kids have been mentored, how many parks have been cleaned up, or how many single moms have been helped through the efforts of their church. Obviously, many missional churches measure how many new believers are being baptized and are joining them on their mission.

Each church will have to decide on its own measures. What missional churches have in common is that they key their measurements to the mission God has given them in their specific context.

Missional leadership

Churches seeking to grow in a missional orientation require a different kind of leadership. Traditionally, churches have preferred pastors and leaders who excel at teaching, caring, and organizing. Such churches have viewed the job of church leadership to entail meeting the needs of and seeking the spiritual growth of those already in the church. For example, the churches I have served have periodically evaluated my performance as a pastor. Not once in these evaluations have they ever asked me whether I am building relationships with, serving, or sharing my faith with those outside the church. While they are certainly glad that I am doing these things, this omission reflects their unconscious assumption that my responsibility to be their "shepherd" only applies to those already within the church. How different this is from the Good Shepherd who said he had sheep who were not yet part of this sheep pen whom he must bring in also (John 10:16).

Churches seeking to be missional need leaders who are able to lead them out into mission. Jesus did not stay in the midst of a circle of believers, training and discipling them in hopes that some of them would go out and reach others. Rather, Jesus took the lead in pursuing God's mission, discipling those who followed him into it. Likewise, missional leaders must lead by example and learn to equip their congregations for mission in the context of that mission, rather than in the safety of a Sunday school classroom.

An elder in our church previously belonged to a missional church in Spain. This church regularly and intentionally spent time together in the cafés, parks, and clubs of their city. As they gathered in these spaces, they encouraged one another spiritually while also befriending those they met and including them in the warmth of their community. Some of these new friends were drawn into a relationship with Jesus as a result. Not surprisingly, this process was messy, as the lifestyles and habits of the newcomers came into conflict with the teachings of Jesus. Yet, the church's leaders patiently worked through these issues with their people, counseling, mentoring, and training as they went. As our elder put it, this was "feet on the ground" training for mission and ministry.

Few of today's pastors and church leaders have been trained to give this sort of leadership. Some are not naturally gifted for it. This is because for so long churches have valued those with pastoral and teaching gifts while overlooking those gifted at sharing their faith and pioneering new endeavors. Can leaders raised and trained in non-missional contexts and methods learn to lead missionally? They certainly can, especially if they make it a point to learn from and invite onto their teams those with evangelistic and other pioneering-type gifts.

Missional practices

Missional churches also have certain practices which set them apart. While there is no list of definitive missional practices, several common ones include discernment, reconciliation, hospitality, communion, and baptism.

Missional churches practice discernment because they are on God's mission, not their own. As Jesus only did what he saw his Father doing (John 5:19), so missional churches need to discern what God is doing around them and how God's Spirit is leading them, rather than proceeding on their own wisdom alone.

Missional churches also prioritize reconciliation. They recognize that they must practice and model among themselves the good news of forgiveness and grace which they share with others. Therefore, they try hard to work out their differences in healthy and peaceable ways. Where possible, they encourage and help those in the wider community to pursue reconciliation as well.

Further, missional churches practice hospitality. Often this involves eating together and eating with those outside the church. In various ways, they demonstrate the good news that there is always room at God's table for another guest. They do not view their homes or gathering spaces solely as private retreat spaces but also as blessings God has entrusted to them to help others feel welcome. Our church once carried out a building renovation which we dubbed "The Wider Welcome." We made a point to remind ourselves that this welcome must be evident in our hearts and our lives as well as in our building.

Finally, missional churches practice communion and baptism. They gather together around the Lord's table, remembering, sharing, and proclaiming Christ's presence and death, and looking with hope toward his return. They also invite those who desire to follow Jesus to enter publicly and definitively into Christ and his salvation through baptism.

Of course, plenty of churches that are not missional engage in many of these practices, too. What makes missional churches unique is that they understand these and other practices not simply as matters of obedience or as benefits to their church fellowship. Rather, missional churches understand these practices as giving shape and expression to the church's calling to be a prophetic sign and living taste of what life in God's kingdom is like. Where possible and appropriate, missional churches engage in these practices in the midst of the people and places they are on mission to reach.

Missional worship

It is common today to confuse worship with worship services. Few realize that the New Testament rarely uses the word "worship" to describe what the early believers did when they gathered together. In the Bible, rather, worship has to do with posturing ourselves and our lives under the authority, majestic greatness, and wonderful goodness of God. Worship involves allegiance, submission, and service as well as adoration and praise. Worship is certainly expressed through song, prayer, sacrifice, sacrament, teaching, and ritual, but it is much more than these. Saying worship is humanity's most important purpose, as many churches do, but then reducing worship to participation in a worship service is to invite idolatry. In fact, in many churches the worship service has become an idol which stands in the way of Christ's will for his people. Jesus warns us in Luke 6:46 not to call him "Lord, Lord" but fail to do what he says. Yet, too many churches never get around to making disciples, caring for the needy, working for justice, or sharing the good news of the gospel, because they are busy pouring their time, energy, finances, and efforts into their worship services.

In missional theology, worship is a political act.[4] In a world that holds national security and prosperity, the global economy, and individual fulfillment as ultimate priorities, the church's worship entails a rejection of these and other idols and a recognition that Jesus alone is Lord. As we prioritize the Lord and his kingdom over all, and experience and participate in the Lord's goodness, we are motivated to express his worth to him and to others. This may take many forms aside from worship services.

Yet, missional churches are certainly not against worship services. When we do gather for worship, our services will both fuel and flow out of our participation in God's mission. We will remember who God is and what God has done for us in Christ. We will remind one another that our ultimate allegiance is to Christ and his glorious purposes, and we will encourage and equip one another to this end. We will also celebrate who God is and what

4. Guder, *Missional Church*, 119.

God is doing in and through us, and we will cry out to God for help and comfort when the battle gets difficult.

For missional churches, therefore, a worship service is as much a thermometer as a thermostat. That is, we do not depend heavily on these services to accomplish the church's purpose and to raise the spiritual temperature of the congregation. We do not assume that every church goal can be accomplished and every church problem solved through the right sermon series. Certainly, worshipping together and hearing God's word taught and expounded are important, but missional churches realize that what happens in the worship service is in many ways a result and overflow of the life and activity of God's people the rest of the week. Are God's people experiencing a vital, growing relationship with Christ, relating to one another with warmth, care, and support, and seeing God's kingdom gain ground in their communities as they engage together in mission? If so, these realities will be evident when we gather together for a worship service. Are our worship services feeling dull and uninspired? Perhaps the solution is not to try harder to jazz them up. More likely, we should recognize that the spiritual temperature of our church is falling and look elsewhere for solutions.

Now that we have explored what missional is and is not, we are faced with the question, is it worth it? What is to be gained by becoming missional and what is the cost of doing so? In the next chapter, we will consider what becoming missional entails as well as what we forfeit when we fail to become missional.

Questions for Discussion or Reflection

- What struck you from this chapter?
- On a scale of 1 to 10, to what extend do you have a missional attitude? What factors have encouraged or discouraged this attitude?

- Does the first figure in this chapter (figure 2) or the second (figure 3) in this chapter better represent your church (or a church you used to attend)? In what ways?

- Which leaders in your church, Christian group, or network are (or could be) the most missional? Why?

- How many of the missional characteristics described in this chapter does your church or Christian group possess?

- Which of the missional characteristics stands out as the most important for you or your church to develop?

- What action will you take in response to what you learned in this chapter?

CHAPTER 6

The Cost of (Not) Becoming Missional

JESUS NEVER SAID FOLLOWING him would be easy. He has called his disciples to follow him into storms, servanthood, self-denial, persecutions, and even the shame and death of the cross. Jesus also insists that through all of this we will experience life abundantly. He promises that "whoever loses their life for my sake will find it" (Matt 10:39). We cannot experience the glory and power of Easter unless we go through the surrender and death of Good Friday. Thus, following Jesus into all he has for us requires that we trust him. Becoming missional definitely requires much faith. It comes with a number of costs, yet Jesus can turn each one into an abundant blessing.

The cost of becoming a learner again

A couple of years ago, I took up Taekwondo as a middle-aged man. At that time, I was also finishing up my doctoral thesis on mission and discipleship. Even while academically I was enjoying elevation to the status of expert in my field, every Saturday morning I put on my white belt and joined the ranks of beginners at the local community center. Anyone seeking to become missional will likewise need to embrace the status of beginner. There is comfort and satisfaction in being good at what we do. It is gratifying when others seek us out to learn from us. However, becoming missional requires we give all that up and humbly become learners again.

For those of us who have been Christians and even church leaders for decades, it is easy to forget that we are first and foremost disciples. To be a disciple is to be a learner, and followers of Jesus are never meant to outgrow this humble posture. The decision to become missional will thrust us back there again. We will need to learn new skills, new perspectives, and new life patterns. Our churches will need to learn new ways of thinking, new strategies, and new processes.

As I have helped church leaders make the missional transition, I have seen many of them humbly and courageously adopt the posture of beginners. I have also seen them be rewarded for doing so, as their stale and weary efforts were replaced with the fresh excitement of new ideas and possibilities. I remember the testimony one church leader with over fifty years of ministry experience shared at the end of the two-year learning community process on mission and discipleship offered by 3DM. He beamed as he described the new joy, challenge, and anticipation missional living was giving him. He described how a couple years before, he had not known anybody in his neighborhood. Now he was building relationships with a half-dozen neighbors and was finding opportunities to share God's love with them. He also told how his level of expectation had risen regarding how God is at work around him. He is enjoying a new openness and eagerness to see how his plans will be interrupted by God, as God continues to do surprising and exciting work around and through him.

The cost of experiencing failure

Biologists have long recognized that organisms unable to adapt to changes in their environment are unlikely to survive. A similar dynamic holds true for businesses and other organizations. In today's environment of rapid social and economic change, the business mantra has become *innovate or die.* Missional thinking recognizes that this reality holds true for churches as well.

In response, some Christians may protest that God will not let his own people go extinct. Surely, if we simply and faithfully hold on to the true Word of God, we can trust God to take care of the rest. Despite its pretense of faith, this attitude is often motivated by an underlying fear of change and a desire to maintain our own comfort. It assumes that God will suspend the laws of the universe to avoid inconveniencing us. Church history is quite clear that God seldom takes this approach. Most often, God's Spirit seeks to preserve his people by guiding us in the changes we must make to survive and thrive in changing times. Those churches that refuse to follow the Spirit in these new directions eventually die off. This observation is not intended to justify compromise or cultural accommodation. Certainly, we must hold true to God's word. Yet, God's people have often had to find ways to translate and re-contextualize that word for new situations. Missional churches believe that we can count on God's Spirit to teach us how to do just that.

Change and innovation involve a great deal of experimentation and failure. Trying something new means risking failure, especially when what we are attempting does not follow the well-worn paths of conventionality. Consider America's history. The pioneers who struck out for the West faced a greater risk of failing than those who stayed behind in well-settled Eastern towns. Without the pioneers' gutsy endeavors, where would our nation be today? Similarly, Thomas Edison experimented with hundreds of materials before he found a filament suitable for manufacturing incandescent light bulbs. To become missional is to choose to experiment, and to risk and experience failure.

In our church, we are attempting to create a culture where innovation is celebrated. We encourage people to experiment and affectionately refer to certain ministry efforts as "research and development" initiatives. We remind our people that no experiment is really a failure as long as we learn something from it. Becoming missional requires that we get comfortable with plenty of failure.

The cost of lowering life-church boundaries

Being missional is a way of life. It cannot be done on Sunday mornings and Wednesday evenings alone. Missional living must be worked out in our daily and weekly rhythms, in how and where we eat, play, relax, live, and work. It requires that we invite people into our lives and get involved in theirs. For those used to having strict boundaries between church and the rest of life, this can be challenging. It can be especially difficult for pastors and other paid church staff.

Many pastors have been taught that strong boundaries between their church and private lives are necessary to maintain emotional and spiritual health. After all, church ministry can be draining and all-consuming. After a long day or week at work, everyone needs to be able to clock out for a while. We need time away from the boss, away from the stresses, expectations, and demands of work. We need time to do what we want to do and the freedom to do it with whomever we choose.

As a pastor, I understand the reasons for boundaries. I have driven my child to an activity on my day off and wound up having a stressful conversation with a church member whose child was also there. I have gone to a Super Bowl party and spent much of the evening listening to a church attender's problems. I have gone out for dinner with friends and spent the evening discussing a difficult church issue with another church leader who was there. It is difficult for those in paid ministry to get away from the expectation that they be always present to care, to listen, and to help.

Nevertheless, leading missionally requires leading in the midst of everyday life. As missional consultant David Rhodes has put it, missional leaders must learn to "lead from our kitchen tables" as well as from our pulpits and offices. Here is the reason why: church leaders cannot expect others to live a life we are not living. We must learn to live it first. We have got to *be* what we want to *see*. Further, others must be able to see us living this way. It is difficult for them to become what they have never seen. The missional life cannot be learned from a sermon series or seminar. It must be experienced and modeled. We as leaders must lead by example.

This kind of leadership does not require that we abandon boundaries altogether. However, it requires we adjust our boundaries in at least two ways. First, we will have to let some people in. We will need to prayerfully select a small group of people to whom we give greater access to our personal lives. Second, instead of placing boundaries on when and where people have access to us, we will need to develop some boundaries regarding what sort of access they have. For example, I once had a group of friends who attended the church I pastored. Periodically, we would all go out for a guys' night. One of them blessed me immensely by setting this boundary: no talking about church stuff on guys' nights. Spiritual conversation was okay, as long as I was viewed as one of the guys and not as the resident expert. This boundary allowed me to share my life with these friends while still providing me with a much-needed break from the role of pastor. The friend who established this boundary later said that I was the best pastor he ever had. Ironically, I suspect it was the boundary he set for me which allowed me to have such a significant impact on his life.

The cost of losing volunteers

As a pastor, I have always communicated to my congregations that service for Christ outside of church is just as valuable as service within. When congregants realize that I really mean this, some express relief and excitement. For years, they had felt a certain call tugging on their hearts, yet their church always sent the message that if they really wanted to serve God, they would do it in the church. Freed from this sense of guilty obligation, a number went on to start exciting outreaches and other ministries. However, their personal freedom and the fruit it bore came at a cost to the church. These volunteers were no longer available to staff existing church ministries. Let's face it, churches always need more help. There are so many needs and so few volunteers and resources to go around. When people and resources are reallocated for mission, fewer are left for existing ministries.

There is no easy way around this dilemma, and cutting existing ministries is seldom a good option. When ministries are cut to make room for mission, those who loved those ministries naturally feel resentful toward the mission efforts which are taking their place. Consider the analogy of a vegetable garden. I have seldom found it fruitful to dig up existing ministries in order to make room for new ones. It works much better to sow new ones among the existing ministries and to see what happens. If the new ministries grow and thrive, they may, in time, shade out some of the existing ones, causing them to die a natural death. Granted, while this gentle approach works well in the long-run, in the short run, it leaves all ministries competing for limited resources. This lack of volunteers and resources must be endured, with as much patience and grace as possible. It is an unavoidable cost of becoming missional.

The cost of lower attendance

When a church shifts its emphasis in the direction of mission, some people may leave. In today's consumer climate, many people choose a church because of what it can offer them. If some of these benefits are withdrawn or attenders are challenged to contribute rather than to receive, some will move on. This is to be expected, though it is never easy. What many churches have found, though, is that a smaller group of motivated, committed disciples can actually accomplish far more than a large group of half-hearted consumers. With the naysayers and foot-draggers gone, those who remain are free to move forward together.

The cost of slow results

 Caesar Kalinowski wrote a book about becoming missional entitled *Small Is Big, Slow Is Fast.* Caesar is right. I have heard church experts say that changing a church culture typically takes five to eight years. Becoming missional is not a quick fix, but rather a wholesale change of culture and orientation. It takes patience and perseverance. There may be few immediate results to encourage us that we are on the right track. As consultants from 3DM, who have helped hundreds of churches make this transition, like to say: "Trust the process" because you are making a "revolutionary change at an evolutionary pace." More than the process, we will have to trust God. If mission is the heartbeat of God and God's great purpose in history, then we have every reason to believe that the God who calls us to make this change will cause it to bear fruit in time.

The cost of change

All of the costs described above will mean change in your life and your church. While some people thrive on change, most people avoid it. Many react to change with feelings of fear, insecurity, and stress. Some in the church will also experience grief as old and beloved ways are left behind. All of these negative emotions squeeze people, and when people are squeezed, negative responses and conflicts can result. Of course, if change is difficult for those experiencing it, it can be even more difficult for those leading it. While change can be managed more or less well, there is no way to avoid its stresses and challenges completely. It is a cost which must be faced to get to the goodness on the other side.

 Having reviewed the costs of becoming missional, we must also consider the costs of not doing so. In chapter 1, we saw that churches can become anemic and lifeless if they fail to believe the faith they proclaim and if they avoid the adventure into which God is calling them. Such churches will not attract many people to themselves or to Jesus. Rather than retaining, attracting, and raising up the younger generation, these churches may become irrelevant or even a source of discouragement to them. Have you noticed young people are not flocking to most churches?

In chapter 2, we saw that the biblical story is the story of God's mission to this world, a mission in which God is seeking to involve all his people. To fail to embrace this mission is to miss the main point of God's Word and to be profoundly out of sync with God and what God is doing in the world. It is to co-opt God's salvation for our own purposes. May God have mercy on us!

In chapter 3, we saw that the Western world is changing, becoming increasingly post-Christian. The time is quickly coming when churches will need to become missional simply to survive, let alone to grow and impact our communities. The forms of church which sustained us in the past are quickly becoming irrelevant and obsolete. If we do not rediscover our purpose and calling, the West will continue to be enveloped in the growing darkness of paganism. As John Stott has famously pointed out in his teachings on the Sermon on the Mount, it makes no sense to blame the darkness for being dark. Rather, what we Christians must ask is: Where is our light? Why are we not shining?[1]

The cost of not becoming missional is great. Yet, the rewards for doing so are even greater. As I have worked with churches earnestly attempting to become missional, I have seen the light come back into the eyes of tired pastors. I have heard their longing to get off the treadmill of trying to meet endless needs and to manage religious machinery. I have sensed leaders' hunger to be used by God again to see lives transformed. I myself have known the joy of investing several years of my life in people and seeing them grow and mature to the point where they began to do the same for others. I have seen congregants with outreach-oriented gifts, who never knew where or if they belonged in the church, finally come alive as they were empowered to lead others in creative outreaches. Above all, God is pleased when his people join him in the mission to which he has committed himself for all of history. To become missional is to enjoy God's pleasure and to further God's glory. In the final chapter, we will explore ways to begin this adventure.

1. See, e.g., Stott, *Sermon on the Mount,* 65 which makes the same point using the analogy of salt and rotten meat.

Questions for Discussion or Reflection

- What struck you from this chapter?

- As you think about Jesus's life and ministry, what risks, costs, and apparent failures did he face, and how did he trust his Father with these?

- What risks have you or your church taken for the sake of God's mission? How did it turn out?

- Change is never easy. If you are part of a church, do the leaders of your church know how to lead change? If not, what resources are you aware of to help them learn?

- For you or your church, what would be the biggest costs of becoming more missional? What would be the biggest costs of *not* doing so?

- Which of the costs described in this chapter feels the hardest for you personally to pay? Why? What would it look like for you to trust God in this area?

- What action will you take in response to what you learned in this chapter?

CHAPTER 7

Ten Missional First Steps

LET'S SAY YOU ARE convinced that being missional is both what the Bible calls us to and what is necessary for the church to be effective in today's culture. Despite the costs involved, you are ready to give it a try. Where do you start? The stereotypical way for a church to "go missional" is to cancel the worship service one Sunday and to do a service project instead. Beginning this way almost guarantees that a lot of folks get upset and are instantly prejudiced against anything missional. A similarly poor way to begin, if you are a pastor, is to stand up one Sunday and declare that your church is going to become a missional church. It is difficult for those in the pew to imagine and comprehend something they have never seen or experienced. Further, it is not fair to expect them to embrace what they cannot envision or understand.

Rather than talking publicly about becoming missional or making big changes, it is best to start small. Here are ten great ways to begin. They are not numbered, because they are not necessarily meant to be done in sequence. Feel free to begin with whichever ones make the most sense for you. Some are more relevant to church leaders, while others relate to anyone wanting to become missional.

Pray.

It goes without saying that we should begin with prayer. Yet, prayer is such an obvious "given" that we tend to overlook its importance. Jesus gave us few specifics regarding what we should ask for in prayer, so it is significant that he clearly and directly told us to pray that the Lord of the Harvest will send more workers into his harvest field (Luke 10:2). When we pray for God's mission, we can pray with confidence and anticipation because we are joining our hearts with God for a purpose in which God passionately delights. We must also continually remind ourselves that if God's kingdom is to come in our local community in tangible and transformative ways, far more power and grace will be required than we are capable of. We desperately need God's power to visit us from on high.

A couple in my church and I have recently begun exploring the possibility of starting a new missional community together. We felt drawn to working together, but we only had a vague notion that our mission might involve something to do with feeding those who are hungry. We were also aware of several practical obstacles related to where we live and work which might make partnering together difficult. So, we began to pray. We asked God specifically to answer three questions for us. What should our specific mission be? Where geographically should this mission be located? And who should we invite to join us? Over the next several weeks, we saw the most clear and specific answers to prayer we had experienced in a long time! We each had chance meetings and conversations with people who confirmed our inclination to reach out to and help those who are hungry, and we were directed to focus on the needs in a specific nearby town. Now we are simply asking who should join us on this mission, expecting that God will make this clear to us also.

This recent experience of answered prayer has reminded me that when we step into what is on God's heart, his power and presence go with us and before us. That is not to say that mission will always go smoothly and easily if we pray. Sometimes we must persevere in prayer for a long time before answers come. Sometimes we face setbacks and failures along the way, for reasons we may never understand. That is all the more reason that we must pray!

Here are some prayers I have found myself praying as I have followed Jesus into the missional adventure.

> *God, give me, give us, a missional heart. Teach us the missional ways of Jesus. Show us what you are doing around us. Show us who you are preparing to receive and respond to your good news. Raise our expectations for what you want to do in and through us. Protect us from the counterattack of the enemy. Protect the work you have begun; don't let the enemy destroy it. Unify other local pastors and leaders around your mission. Give them a common heart and vision. Breathe your power into our feeble efforts. God, when the world around us is dark and the name of your Son is mocked or ignored, I know this is not what you want. Give your Son the glory he deserves. Cause his light to shine brightly! Thank you that you take great delight in our efforts to engage in your mission!*

Go first.

When I was a new pastor, I wanted to equip the people in my congregation for ministry and mission. I assumed I could do this through sermons, Bible studies, and Sunday school lessons. After all, this is what I had been trained and hired to do. They were the ones out in the world every day, at work and in their neighborhoods. My job was to care for and train them, and if I did this well enough, they would go out and change the world. It took me several years to realize that this center-out approach would never work.

First of all, learning about missional living in a classroom on Sunday mornings did not help people live it out during the week. Going from information to implementation was too big of a leap. They needed example and involvement as well. They needed me to show them how it was done and to be there in real time to coach them through the details and nuances.

Second, as I remained cloistered within the church, I became increasingly out of touch with the culture I was seeking to equip my congregation to reach. Sharing my faith with people outside the church became more of a memory than a current reality. As a result, I became less effective in helping my congregation to engage relevantly with the people around them.

Third, the more people followed my example, the less missional they actually became. After all, the example I was giving them to emulate was that of someone who spent all his time with church people! They concluded that mature Christians must spend all their time at church.

Contrast my first attempts at missional leadership with that of Jesus. Jesus did not huddle disciples around him and then send them out on mission while he stayed home. Rather, he led the way in mission, calling his disciples to join him as he went. In this way, he could naturally lead by example and provide on-the-job coaching for those he was training. Jesus was a brilliant leader!

If you are a church leader wanting to lead your church in becoming missional, do not attempt to preach or organize your congregation into this transformation. The best way you can begin is to learn to be more missional yourself. Others cannot become what they cannot see. They need someone to show them the way. They need to see a missional life and to hear stories with which they can relate. This does not mean you must be a perfect example of missional living before you invite others to follow. People do not need a perfect example, but they do need to see a living one.[1] As you develop stories of your own successes, as well as failures, you will be able to speak with authority and credibility as you seek to lead others.

Get trained.

It took me a long time to realize that I could not figure out how to become missional simply by attending another conference or reading another book. Trust me, I tried! Maybe you have tried the conference-and-book approach, too. After all, this is how ministry success is typically marketed to us. Attend this

1. Breen, *Discipling Culture*, 60.

conference, buy this book, and you can succeed just like the big-name speaker or writer did.

The truth is that most things in life cannot be learned this way. Becoming missional certainly cannot, for two reasons. First, it is too revolutionary of a change. Becoming missional changes everything. It requires new ways of thinking, new instincts, new reflexes, and new habits. These changes cannot take place all at once, and the tendency to revert to old patterns is strong and inevitable. Before long, that book or conference which was so inspiring has become a distant memory. If we are going to fight inertia and sustain the kind of change required to become missional, something more is needed.

Second, becoming missional looks somewhat different in every context. There is no single model or formula which fits every situation. Your context has a different history, different culture, different mix of opportunities and barriers, and a different set of strengths and gifts compared to any other. Therefore, only you can become the expert in what being missional should look like in your context. A conference speaker or author who does not know your context cannot possibly do this work for you.

To become missional, we must therefore commit ourselves to becoming learners again. We must seek out those who know more than we do and devote ourselves to several years of walking with them, receiving their training and coaching. In selecting a missional mentor from which to learn, beware of anyone offering you the one perfect model. What you need instead is someone who can teach you principles and strategies and coach you in how to contextualize these to your situation.

There are some excellent training resources available through missional practitioners like Caesar Kalinowski, 3DM, and Future Travelers. Oh, and by all means, do read books as well. After all, I wrote one! Neil Cole, Mike Breen, Hugh Halter, Caesar Kalinowski, and others have written excellent books on living missionally. An annotated reading list of books, websites, and blogs is provided at the end of this book.

Disciple others.

Most people will never be able to live truly missional lives until they have been discipled. This fact is so important and so often overlooked that it is worth repeating. *Most people will never be able to live truly missional lives until they have been discipled.* Did you hear that? If we want our lives to become missional, we must seek out discipleship. If we want to see our churches become missional, we must disciple people into it. We *must* prioritize the making of disciples.

This is what Jesus did. He devoted three years to investing in a small group of disciples. He taught them the missional skills he possessed. He shaped their characters and outlooks to be like his. Certainly, Jesus taught them much more than how to be missionaries. But he did not teach them less than this. For Jesus, every disciple was to be a missional disciple. Every one of his followers was to be a missionary. That is why discipleship is inherent in the Great Commission. Jesus said, "Therefore go and make disciples of all nations, baptizing them . . . and teaching them to obey everything I have commanded you" (Matt 28:18–20). To be a disciple of Jesus is to make disciples, and to be a disciple is to be missional.

Living missionally requires that we develop new skills and grow in our character. These are best gained through intentional discipling relationships. This is why you needed to become a learner first. Now, you will need to disciple others who are open to learning from you. Consider pulling together a small group of others who respect you and are hungry or at least open to exploring the missional adventure you are on. Share your life with them. Teach them what you are learning. Take risks and engage in missional experiments with them. Have fun trying and exploring. As you learn, grow, and see even small successes together, begin sharing these stories with others.

Rediscover the good news in the gospel.

Does the gospel still sound to you like good news that you want to share? Is it shaping, sweetening, and transforming every area of your life? If not, perhaps it is time to do some personal work, deepening your understanding of the gospel and relating it to your own life.

It used to be that almost everyone believed in God, sin, and hell, and they hoped to go to heaven when they died. Many had a basic assumption that if they lived a fairly moral life, everything would work out for them when they got to the pearly gates. Based on this cultural context, evangelistic ministries developed various simple gospel presentations to clearly explain how Jesus is the way to eternal life. These presentations helped people see that we cannot atone for our sins through our own moral efforts. Then, they shared the good news that Christ has paid the price for our sins, and we need only to be sorry for our sins and to put our faith in Christ to receive eternal life. God has used these simple presentations to bring many to faith in Jesus, myself included. I am personally grateful for them.

Nevertheless, such presentations have two weaknesses. First, they can leave the (false) impression that the gospel only relates to the beginning of the Christian life. While they help us to begin a relationship with God, they offer us little assistance in applying the gospel to every area of our lives. Second, these presentations are less likely to sound like good news to people today. In fact, when we use them, they may not feel like good news to us. This is likely because people today do not believe in sin or worry much about the afterlife. Thus, these presentations give us the uncomfortable task of trying to convince people that they need saving from something they do not even believe exists.

Thankfully, while the gospel is not less than what these gospel presentations communicate, it is far more! The gospel introduces us to the amazing and attractive person Jesus who can not only forgive our sins but can also teach us what a truly human life looks like, heal our diseases and brokenness, set us free from all that holds us captive, and lead us into a wonderful relationship with God his Father. This Jesus died to show us how much God loves us as well as to take away all our guilt and shame. He then rose again, having conquered death, to pave the way into a new creation and eternal life. Even now, Jesus is establishing God's kingdom in which all things are being restored, redeemed, healed, and made new. One day Jesus will return to finish the job! All that and more are offered in the gospel.

The gospel contains good news for every area of our lives. It invites us again and again to stop relying on our own moral track record for our security and identity, and to step deeper and further into the grace and love of God. As we come to more deeply understand and trust the gospel, we grow more humble, peaceful, thankful, joyful, gracious, and generous. We are relieved of the burdens of having to perform to be acceptable and needing to compare ourselves to others. We are freed to love and to live our lives with the incredible purpose of helping more of God's kingdom to come around us.

If we can rediscover how the gospel is good news for ourselves, it may increase our desire to share it with others. A deeper and fuller understanding of the gospel will also give us flexibility in how we share it, enabling us to express it in ways which sound like good news to those we encounter. To the addict, we will be able to speak of Christ's power to bring freedom and deliverance. To the lonely and dislocated, of the welcome of a new family and home. To the victim of sexual assault, of the assurance that Jesus will cleanse from all shame. To the discouraged activist, of the invitation to join a cause guaranteed to win in the end. To everyone, of the promise that Christ can restore our relationship with the one who Created us and can wash away all of our guilt before him.

This is not to suggest that we may avoid the central gospel tenets that all people have sinned and that our sin separates us from a Holy God. It is rather to recognize that when talking to people who do not believe in sin, offering them a Jesus who forgives sins is unlikely to be a fruitful starting place. Since the gospel contains much more good news about Jesus, we would do better to begin at other points and to cover sin further along, when Jesus's goodness has made them aware of their own sinfulness. After all, this is what Jesus himself did. To the lepers he offered cleansing, to the diseased healing, to the demonized deliverance, to the marginalized welcome. Once they had drawn closer to Jesus and gotten to know him better, some turned away (John 6:66), while others, like Peter, confessed their sins: "Go away from me, Lord; I am a sinful man!" (Luke 5:8). As we explore the richness of the gospel for ourselves, we will be better equipped to lead others toward a life-changing encounter with Jesus.

Learn to contextualize.

I mentioned earlier that after college I moved to Budapest, Hungary to teach at a public high school. One of my two American teammates there was a friend from college. Before long, we found several Christian students at the school who were interested in participating in a Bible study with us. We were excited about this ministry opportunity and glad that our college fellowship had trained us well for this task. We prayerfully picked a Bible passage, studied it ourselves, and then wrote discussion questions just like we had done when we led Bible studies in college. When the Hungarian teens arrived, we fed them cookies and then read the passage together and started asking our discussion questions. Within a few minutes, we noticed them looking at one another sheepishly. Then, they began whispering to one another in Hungarian. Finally, the one who spoke the best English politely explained, "We want you to tell us about the Bible, not to ask us what it means. We don't know. You are the teachers. We are the students."

This was our first lesson in contextualization. As we later learned, the communist-based school system which had educated these young people did not value free and independent thinking or participatory learning. Rather, students were expected to memorize and repeat back what their teachers taught them. These students expected to do the same for us.

This experience forced us to consider whether the participatory, discussion-based method of Bible study we had learned in college was inherently Christian or whether it was merely an American approach to Christianity. When missionaries bring the gospel to a different culture, they are constantly faced with the need to distinguish between what is truly Christian and what is really just cultural. Additionally, they have to learn to communicate their faith in ways which are intelligible and compelling to the culture they are seeking to reach. These are the challenges of contextualization. Because the Western culture around us has shifted so dramatically from the Christian culture still preserved in churches, it is a challenge all who desire to be missional must face.

The best way to begin learning to contextualize is to become a student of the cultural context which you feel called to reach. Start paying attention to what motivates people. What are their dreams and hopes? What are their fears and anxieties? How do they spend their free time and their discretionary income? What does this say about what they value? Also try to understand what they believe. What narratives give meaning to their lives? What do these narratives tell about how life should ideally work, what has gone wrong, and how it might be fixed? What are their religious views? To what moral values do they aspire? What violations of these values do they consider most heinous? What sorts of people do they respect and admire? Why? Also consider their practical circumstances. What do they feel most needs to be fixed or improved in their community? What do they see as their communities' greatest strengths and assets?

Answering these questions will require intense and sympathetic listening. Here are some ways to listen. Take a walk through your community and ask God to show you how God sees it and what God is doing there. Ask questions of people you meet, and really listen to the answers they give you. Reach out to community leaders and ask questions of them. Find out what books/periodicals/social media sources and what movies/TV shows/performances are popular with those in your community. Read and watch them, and pay attention to what they are communicating.

As you listen and get to know the surrounding culture, consider how the gospel critiques it. Then ask yourself whether it is really the gospel critiquing it or your own cultural assumptions critiquing it. Also consider what aspects of the culture the gospel affirms. Every culture has positive, negative, and neutral aspects. It is hard for us to be objective about which are which because our own cultural assumptions cloud our objectivity. Nevertheless, we must try.

Based on our evaluation of the culture, we must then wrestle with how to communicate the gospel in a way which challenges the idolatries of the culture and invites people to find forgiveness and redemption in Christ. We will want to reflect upon which themes of the gospel will particularly resonate with that culture. Is it God's sacrificial love? God's redeeming power? God's willingness to stoop down and come among us? God's payment of the penalty we deserve? God's reconciling heart? These questions will help us shape our telling of the gospel message.

We must also remember that our actions communicate as much as or more than our words. Jesus not only proclaimed the good news of the gospel—he also brought its reality into people's midst. We must ask what prayers we should pray that Jesus might demonstrate the reality of his kingdom to the people around us. We must consider what sort of acts of service or justice and what sort of ministry forms and practices will best communicate and embody the gospel in our context. We must ask what the gospel will look like when it becomes a reality in our local community. Will the hungry be fed, the lonely be loved, the ashamed be honored, the stressed find peace? All of this requires thoughtful and prayerful reflection, creativity, and flexibility. Contextualization is a huge and never-ending task. The sooner we get started, the better.

Experiment.

There is no one way to be missional. You will need to figure out what works for you and your context. Make every effort not to do this alone. Mission is definitely a team sport. Jesus always sent his disciples out in teams of at least two, and he told his followers that it was their love and unity that would show the world the Father sent him. Find a few willing friends to join you, or even better, enlist those you are discipling. If you have a family, involve them to the extent that they are willing, if at all possible.

Once you have found your team, engage in some missional experimentation together. Agree to all hang out at the same coffee house or to join the same gym. Pick a neighborhood to adopt, a park to frequent, or a common hobby to engage in together with other like-minded people. See who you meet and what needs you can meet. Pray together for eyes to see what God is doing there. Expect God to show up and surprise you. Keep your eyes open for the people of peace whom God brings across your path. These are people who like you, welcome you, listen to you, and even serve you (Luke 10:6). Ask God what you should do next to build relationships with these people. Throw parties or organize barbeques and invite them along.

As things begin to happen, share your stories with others. Celebrate your failures. There will be many. They are not actually failures as long as you reflect on what you can learn from them. Each experiment will teach you something valuable and increase your expertise at being missional.

Learn from overseas missionaries.

Does your church support missionaries who serve overseas? Next time they visit your church, invite them to train your congregation in how to do missions. Several years ago, our church invited a missionary couple we support to give us some basic training in how to contextualize the gospel, with illustrations from their ministry overseas. Later, they did another training on "How to think like a missionary." These missionaries felt valued in being able to share their expertise with us, and we felt closer to them as we came to relate to the cross-cultural challenges they face. The whole experience underscored to all of us that we are all missionaries, wherever God has placed us. As the Western church wakes up to this reality, who better to train us for the task than those who have already been on the mission field for years?

Identify others gifted for mission.

Call them evangelists, missionaries, apostles, prophets, activists, or whatever. These are your pioneering types. They may be creative or entrepreneurial, out-of-the-box thinkers or early adopters. They will likely be your greatest allies. Some of them will immediately be excited about what you are trying to do. Others may not get it at first, but as they taste missional living and warm up to it, they will provide the spiritual insight, power, and energy you need. This is what God has gifted them for. One of the great tragedies in the church is that we have very often undervalued and overlooked people with these kinds of gifts. With no place to contribute in the church, they have often gone out and gotten involved in parachurch ministries. In the missional church, these people are valued and called forth. Before long, they are often leading the way. Find these people, share with them what you are learning, and invite them to join you.

Develop life rhythms.

Habits and traditions are powerful. Once we have formed them, they give shape to our lives and allow us to do naturally what we would otherwise have to work hard at remembering to do. I once preached a sermon on the practicalities of living out Jesus's statement that anyone who would follow him must deny themselves and take up their cross daily. I compared it to withdrawing your life savings from the bank and instead of giving it away all at once, giving it away a dollar at a time.[2] As he listened, one professional in our congregation felt nudged by God about the homeless he passed on his way to work each morning. He decided to start carrying a few extra dollars and to ask God each day to guide him in

2. This idea was borrowed from a sermon by Fred Craddock.

how he could give this money away in a manner which would bless these people. That was fifteen years ago, and I no longer pastor that church. I recently caught up with him, however, and he informed me that he is still continuing this practice. Then he recounted the many lessons he has learned about helping those in need and the relationships he has built with people on the streets. He spoke of each person by name and of several of them as friends. He told me how he helped one man fly to another city to attend a family funeral and of the impact it had on this man to reconnect with his family. He also told of how several of his homeless friends have spoken into his life and encouraged him when he was down. All of this became possible because he developed a life rhythm and remained faithful to it.

Consider adding one or two missional rhythms to your life. For example, every morning you could ask God to show you what God is doing that day and where the people of peace are. Or, visit the same restaurant whenever you go out to eat. Choose the same checkout clerk at the grocery store and be friendly to them (even if the line at their register is longer). Work in the front yard or take a walk at the time when most of your neighbors are out. Invite a neighbor over for dinner the first Saturday of every month. Volunteer at the soup kitchen at the same time each week. Simple steps like these, while small in themselves, will add up over time and take you farther than you thought possible.

Lighten your load.

Much of living missionally involves doing what you are already doing with new intentionality. God is already at work around you, and you are now choosing to tune in and to participate. You are seeking to remember that you are a missionary wherever you go and looking for opportunities to bless others and to join in with what God is doing in their lives. However, as missional efforts and opportunities become part of your life, you will also want to reflect on what you might be able to cut out of your life to free up time and energy. What are you doing in the name of rest or recreation which is not actually refreshing or life-giving? What are you doing only because you have not had the courage (or a good enough reason) to say no? What are you doing out of guilt or obligation that God is not really calling you to do? What are you doing as a result of fear rather than from a place of trust in a good God who loves you? These are the places you will want to trim back.

And how about your church? Are there activities you keep doing though no one can remember the reason why anymore? Are there ministries or traditions which no longer serve any significant purpose? It is generally not prudent to kill these ministries, unless they are toxic. Even if they are toxic, they should probably still be honored with a very nice funeral. More likely, ministries which have lost their purpose will need to be politely neglected so that attention and resources can be reallocated to mission.

Do not give up.

The changes you are seeking will likely be small at first. They may come slowly. There will be plenty of failures and setbacks along the way. People you invest in will move away, lose interest, and perhaps even betray you. Shifting a culture takes time, patience, and perseverance. Yet, change experts tell us there is a tipping point when the forces aligned for change outnumber the forces aligned against it. The good news is that the percentage at which the balance tips is actually far less than 50 percent![3] Think of change as turning a fly-wheel. At first, the wheel is very hard, almost impossible, to turn. With great effort, you can barely get it to budge. As it begins to move, it becomes easier to turn; then, easier still. Once it starts turning, it soon becomes hard to stop. This takes time. Change is measured in terms of years, not weeks or months. Do not give up.

Questions for Discussion or Reflection

- What struck you from this chapter?

3. See Gladwell, *Tipping Point*.

- Have you ever read a book or been to a conference that inspired you? Did lasting change result? Why or why not?

- Why is it important for leaders to "go first"?

- Is the gospel still good news in your own heart and life? Why or why not?

- Which two or three steps offered in the chapter would be the best places for you or your church to start?

- Who do you know or where could you find help to assist you in taking these steps?

- What action will you take in response to what you learned in this chapter?

- Review the actions you planned to take after reading previous chapters. How did they go? Are there any you need to revisit?

Why it Will Never Work in Your Context (And How to Succeed Anyway)

As my colleagues and I have helped church leaders work through what it might look like for them to become missional, we have heard a common refrain: "That sounds great for you guys, but it will never work here in our context." "It might be possible to be missional in the Bible belt, but people here are too secular." "Maybe young singles can be missional, but the families in our church are too busy." "A large church probably has the resources to become missional, but our church is too small." You get the idea. Being missional might work for somebody else, but it will never work for you.

Let me give you four scenarios in which being missional will never work in your context. First, it will never work if you give up quickly. It took William Wilberforce over forty-five years to get slavery outlawed in the British Empire. Imagine if he had given up after a year or two. William Carey, known as the Father of Modern Missions, labored as a missionary in India for seven years before he saw his first convert. Imagine if he had given up after five years. Ask any missionary. Missions by its very nature is prone to failures, setbacks, and false starts. Even Jesus saw all his disciples desert him after he had invested in their lives for three years. Imagine if Jesus had given up! If you quit, you will never see the fruit God would eventually have brought.

Second, being missional will never work if you rigidly insist on sticking with your first plan. Mission requires that you experiment, experiment, and experiment. You will need to hold your ideas and strategies loosely and be willing to adapt or change them if they prove to be ineffective. Some friends of mine who formed a missional community spent several years pursuing one outreach idea after another. Each one proved to be a dead-end. Finally, when they were frustrated, discouraged, and fresh out of ideas, God opened a door for them to reach out to refugees who are being resettled in their area. Many other missional communities tell similar stories of failure before success. My present church has been experimenting with ways to be missional in our community for almost ten years. In the first few years, we experienced many false starts. I tried to start a discipleship group to train leaders to be more missional. Nobody had time. We tried to start a community garden. We could not secure a suitable location. We tried to reach parents with young children. The group spearheading it ran out of energy and ideas. We tried to reach the local environmentalist community. Those with this vision got distracted by other things. We tried to reach a local neighborhood. The neighbors showed little interest. It was tempting to give up and conclude, "Being missional just will not work here. People are too secular, too wealthy, too busy." However, we did not give up, and in time God led us to pockets of people who are open to us and to Jesus. We have since established effective outreaches in a neighborhood, a square-dancing club, a local arts community, and a bar/restaurant.

Third, becoming missional will never work if you insist on doing it perfectly from the beginning. I made this mistake early on in my missional journey. I thought my church and my life should look like textbook examples. I did not want to get this wrong, so I held back until the perfect scenario developed (it never did!). Along the way, I passed up a number of opportunities which would have at least gotten us moving in the right direction. There is no magic ministry formula. Life is messy. Ministry is messy. People are messy. Every context is unique, having its own opportunities and impediments. Your life and your church will never be perfectly missional, perfectly loving, perfectly anything. Do not let that fact stop you from proceeding in the direction you sense God calling you to go.

Fourth, being missional will never work unless God cares about the people around you. Yes, I am being cheeky here, but let us not forget that it is God's mission we are talking about. You will never become missional without God's power and a belief that God wants to use you. All around you are people who lack hope, who do not know God's love, and who have nowhere to turn to find help and peace when they are over their heads. All around you are people who are heading toward an eternal destiny separated from the Source of life and love. All around you are families, communities, and workplaces experiencing strife, stress, brokenness, and bondage. If God does not care about these people and these places, then becoming missional will not work.

Let me put it another way. All around you are people who do not recognize Jesus Christ as the Savior and Lord of this world and who do not give him glory. If the Father is okay with these people overlooking and snubbing his own Son, if the Father is okay with them not having an opportunity to benefit from Christ's ultimate sacrifice, then being missional will not work.

On the other hand, what if God does want these people to know his Son? What if God does want Jesus to be glorified in their lives? What if God does want to see people healed and set free? What if God does want people to come and join his family? If so, then by becoming more missional we might just be on the right track. It is time for a faith check. Do you really believe that God "wants all people to be saved" (1 Tim 2:4)? Do you believe that God really wants to answer the prayer "your kingdom come, your will be done, *on earth* as it is in heaven" (Matt 6:10, italics added)? If you do, are you living accordingly? A few years ago, I was wrestling with my own commitment to being missional, given its many challenges. I concluded that I would rather fail trying to accomplish the right thing than succeed at the wrong things.

I have good news, though. Despite the naysayers, failure is by no means inevitable, though it may feel that way at points along the journey. I know small and large churches that have become missional. I know churches in wealthy suburbs and in inner-city neighborhoods. I know churches in the Bible belt and on the secular, urban coasts. I know churches full of twenty-somethings and churches with plenty of busy soccer moms, all of which have become missional.

How can you succeed? It will take a faith commitment to pursue, and to continue to pursue, God's heart. It will require that you not forget or get distracted from the big story of God's word, which is the story of God's unrelenting mission to save this world. It will take a commitment to continually push past good things, in order to pursue the best thing. It will take vigilance, lest you fall back into the comfortable assumption that playing church like we have always done is good enough. As those in the 3DM movement like to remind each other, quoting the title of a Eugene Peterson book, it will take "a long obedience in the same direction."[1]

When Jesus sought to describe what the kingdom of God is like, he did not compare it to the profit chart of a successful corporation that reflects a straightforward, linear increase. Rather, he compared it to a tiny seed which a farmer plants in the ground (Mark 4:26–32). At first, it seems as if the seed does nothing. The farmer goes away, waking and sleeping, unable to control or even understand what is happening under the soil. Yet, in time, the seed grows and produces a huge yield, all by itself it would seem.

In taking steps toward becoming missional, we need to have the attitude of that farmer. Progress may seem small and insignificant at first. We may not be able to draw straight lines between our efforts and the results or lack of results we are seeing. Yet, as we faithfully stay the course, we can labor with the expectation that God will indeed accomplish his mission. After all, this has been God's committed purpose all through history and the purpose for which he sent his own beloved Son. In the end, God gets all the glory. What we get is the satisfaction and joy of playing a role in so grand an endeavor.

---

1. Peterson, *Long Obedience*.

For Further Reading

Breen, Mike. *Building a Discipling Culture: How to Release a Missional Movement by Discipling People Like Jesus Did*, 3rd ed. Pawleys Island, SC: 3DM, 2017. A great and practical introduction on how to be a missional disciple and to disciple others for mission.

Breen, Mike. *Covenant and Kingdom: The DNA of the Bible*. Pawleys Island, SC: 3DM, 2010. An easy-to-read tracing of the themes of covenant and kingdom (mission) through the biblical story.

Breen, Mike & Sally. *Family on Mission: Integrating Discipleship into the Fabric of our Everyday Lives*, 2nd ed. Pawleys Island, SC: 3DM, 2018. A practical vision for living a life of mission in community with others.

Breen, Mike. *Leading Kingdom Movements: The "Everyman" Notebook on How to Change the World*. Pawleys Island, SC: 3DM, 2013. A big picture vision of what it can look like for Christianity to be a missional movement instead of a religious institution.

Cole, Neil. *Organic Church: Growing Faith Where Life Happens*. San Francisco: Jossey-Bass, 2005. An inspiring roadmap on how to develop a very incarnation and missional form of church.

Frost, Michael. *The Road to Missional: Journey to the Center of the Church*. Grand Rapids: Baker, 2011. A challenging and inspiring reconsideration of what Scripture says about what God is doing in the world and where we fit in.

Halter, Hugh and Matt Smay. *The Tangible Kingdom: Creating Incarnational Community, The Posture and Practices of Ancient Church Now*. San Francisco: Jossey-Bass, 2008. A modern classic on living and doing church missionally.

Halter, Hugh and Matt Smay. *The Tangible Kingdom Primer: An 8-week Guide to Incarnational Community*, 2nd ed. Missio, 2009. A study guide-style exploration of how to live a life of mission.

Kalinowski, Caesar. *The Gospel Primer: An 8-Week Guide to Transformation in Community*. Missio, 2013. A study guide-style exploration of the gospel and how it applies to our lives.

Kalinowski, Caesar. *Transformed: A New Way of Being Christian*. Grand Rapids: Zondervan, 2014. A vision and description of how to live missionally with others illustrated by many inspiring stories.

Keller, Timothy. *Center Church: Doing Balanced Gospel-Center Ministry in Your City*. Grand Rapids: Zondervan, 2012. An excellent text on what the gospel is and how churches can contextualize it, particularly for urban areas.

McNeal, Reggie. *Missional Renaissance: Changing the Scorecard for the Church*. San Francisco: Jossey-Bass, 2009. An exploration of how churches can shift from measuring attendance to measuring missional impact.

Pfeiffer, Eric. *Missional Communities Leader Guide: Starting, Growing, and Multiplying Your Missional Groups*. Pawleys Island, SC: 3DM, 2016. A practical guide for starting and leading missional communities which includes months' worth of ideas/content for gatherings.

Robertson, Dwight. *You Are God's Plan A: There Is No Plan B*, 2nd ed. Colorado Springs: David C. Cook, 2010. A simple vision for living a missional life illustrated with many inspiring stories.

Wright, Christopher J. H. *The Mission of God's People: A Biblical Theology of the Church's Mission*. Grand Rapids: Zondervan, 2010. An exploration of the theme of mission in the Bible.

www.3dmovements.com. Information on 3DM's training and coaching as well as resources, weekly emails, and links to other missional blogs.

www.3dmstand.com. Lots of missional ideas and resources particularly for women, but often applicable to everyone.

www.caesarkalinowski.com. Blogs, videos, training courses, weekly emails, and other resources on how to live missionally.

www.vergenetwork.org. Blogs, videos, weekly emails, and other resources on how to live missionally.

Do you have questions, ideas, or thoughts about the journey to becoming missional? Keep the conversation going. Visit Dick's author page on Facebook or email him at missional@disciples.com.

About the Author

OVER THE PAST FIFTEEN years, Dick has been helping the two churches he's pastored become more missional, one near Vancouver, Canada and the other in New York. As a certified coach and frontier leader with the 3DM missional discipleship movement, he has also helped dozens of churches in the Northeast United States reorient themselves toward mission and discipleship.

Dick has a DMin in discipleship and mission from Northern Seminary (Lombard, Illinois) and an MDiv from Regent College (Vancouver, British Columbia). Prior to seminary, he spent three years doing missions work in Budapest, Hungary and three more in Washington, DC. In DC, Dick trained urban humanitarian leaders at the Congressional Hunger Center and helped start a multi-ethnic church.

Dick is passionate about discipleship, cultivating rich, biblical community (*oikos*), Biblical Studies, and great coffee. He and his wife Anne have four great kids whom they homeschool.

Bibliography

Breen, Mike. *Building a Discipling Culture: How to Release a Missional Movement by Discipling People Like Jesus Did*, 3rd ed. Pawleys Island, SC: 3DM, 2017.

Gladwell, Malcolm. *The Tipping Point: How Little Things Can Make a Big Difference.* Boston: Back Bay, 2002.

Guder, Darrell L, ed. *Missional Church: A Vision for the Sending of the Church in North America.* Grand Rapids: Eerdmans, 1998.

Harkins, Greg L. and Cally Parkinson, *Reveal: Where Are You?* Barrington, IL: Willow Creek Association, 2007.

Kalinowski, Caesar. "Who Broke the Missional Movement?" http://www.caesarkalinowski.com/broke-missional-movement.

Kreider, Alan. *The Change of Conversion and the Origin of Christendom.* Harrisburg, PA: Trinity, 1999.

Peterson, Eugene H. *A Long Obedience in the Same Direction: Discipleship in an Instant Society.* Downers Grove, IL: InterVarsity, 2000.

Roxburgh, Alan J. "The Missional Church." *Theology Matters* 10 (September/October 2004) 1–5. http://www.theologymatters.com/SepOct04.pdf.

Spurgeon, C. H. "A Sermon and a Reminiscence." *Sword and Trowel* (March 1973). http://www.biblebb.com/files/spurgeon/srmn1873.htm.

Stark, Rodney. *The Rise of Christianity: How the Obscure, Marginal Jesus Movement Became the Dominant Religious Force in the Western World in a Few Centuries.* San Francisco: Harper, 1997.

Stott, John R. W. *The Message of the Sermon on the Mount.* The Bible Speaks Today. Downers Grove, IL: InterVarsity, 1978.

Tickle, Phyllis. *The Great Emergence: How Christianity Is Changing and Why.* Grand Rapids: Baker, 2012.

Wright, Christopher J. H. *The Mission of God's People: A Biblical Theology of the Church's Mission.* Grand Rapids: Zondervan, 2010.

Made in the USA
Columbia, SC
09 January 2023

75842668R00065